GIRLFRIEND
Greetings

NORTH LIGHT BOOKS
CINCINNATI, OHIO
www.artistsnetwork.com

Girlfriend Greetings. Copyright © 2006 by North Light Books. Manufactured in China. All rights reserved. The patterns and drawings in the book are for personal use of the reader. By permission of the designer and publisher, they may be either hand-traced or photocopied to make single copies, but under no circumstances may they be resold or republished. It is permissible for the purchaser to make the projects contained herein and sell them at fairs, bazaars and craft shows. No other part of this book may be reproduced in any form or by any electronic or mechanical means including information storage and retrieval systems without permission in writing from the publisher, except by a reviewer, who may quote a brief passage in review. Published by North Light Books, an imprint of F+W Publications, Inc., 4700 East Galbraith Road, Cincinnati, Ohio 45236. (800) 289-0963. First edition.

10 09 08 07   5 4 3 2

Distributed in Canada by Fraser Direct
100 Armstrong Avenue
Georgetown, ON, Canada L7G 5S4
Tel: (905) 877-4411

Distributed in the U.K. and Europe by David & Charles
Brunel House, Newton Abbot, Devon, TQ12 4PU, England
Tel: (+44) 1626 323200, Fax: (+44) 1626 323319
E-mail: mail@davidandcharles.co.uk

Distributed in Australia by Capricorn Link
P.O. Box 704, S. Windsor, NSW 2756 Australia
Tel: (02) 4577-3555

Library of Congress Cataloging-in-Publication Data
Girlfriend greetings : 60 cards to make & give /
Edited by Christine Doyle.
     p. cm.
  Includes index.
  ISBN-13: 978-1-58180-862-9 (alk. paper)
  ISBN-10: 1-58180-862-3
  1. Greeting cards. I. Doyle, Christine.
  TT872.G57 2006
  745.594'1--dc22
                                        2006009428

Editor: Christine Doyle
Designers: Marissa Bowers and Stephanie Goodrich
Layout Artist: Kathy Gardner
Production Coordinator: Greg Nock
Photographers: Hal Barkan and Christine Polomsky

Metric Conversion Chart

TO CONVERT	TO	MULTIPLY BY
Inches	Centimeters	2.54
Centimeters	Inches	0.4
Feet	Centimeters	30.5
Centimeters	Feet	0.03
Yards	Meters	0.9
Meters	Yards	1.1
Sq. Inches	Sq. Centimeters	6.45
Sq. Centimeters	Sq. Inches	0.16
Sq. Feet	Sq. Meters	0.09
Sq. Meters	Sq. Feet	10.8
Sq. Yards	Sq. Meters	0.8
Sq. Meters	Sq. Yards	1.2
Pounds	Kilograms	0.45
Kilograms	Pounds	2.2
Ounces	Grams	28.3
Grams	Ounces	0.035

Acknowledgments

A huge thank you to all the designers who contributed their talents to this book. Without girlfriends like you, this project would not have been possible.

Anna Armendariz

Linda Beeson

Miki Benedict

Jeanette Beshears

Cindy Curtis

Tonia Davenport

Jennifer Ellefson

Kelly Anne Grundhauser

Nicole Jackson

Anabelle O'Malley

Stacey Stamitoles

Kristen Swain

Judi Watanabe

Teresa Wilkins

Sherry Wright

Contents

precious

YOUR
FRIENDSHIP

CONGRATS

Girlfriend Power

You know who they are. Your bestest friends. The ones you turn to time and again. The people who help you through life, and you do the same for them. You've known one since grade school, met another in college, and another was your neighbor when you bought your first house. Your girlfriends.

The crux of a girlfriend relationship is that you do things for each other, because that's what girlfriends do. You cheer them up when they're down and cheer them on when they're making a move. You give them advice and you listen to theirs. You let them know just how fun they are.

For all those things, and more, there's a card to express it here in *Girlfriend Greetings*. Admit it—no one appreciates a handmade card like your girlfriends. They know how much it means to get a card you made, and it'll make them feel great, besides.

In sections like Bad Hair Days, Glam It Up!, It's All About You, You Go, Girl!, and Best Friends Forever, you'll find the perfect sentiment for any occasion.

If you haven't done a lot (or any) cardmaking before, flip to the How'd She Do That? section of techniques on page 86. There you'll find step-by-step photos showing how to ink a stamp, use rub-on transfers, and more. It's a snap!

Bad Hair Days

Who couldn't use a little
pick-me-up once in a while?
Whether your friend is going
through a messy breakup, is
having a hard time at work,
or just got a very unfortunate
haircut, there's a card in the
pages that follow to boost her
spirits and let her know you're
there to see her through.

Girl Talk

STACEY STAMITOLES

WHAT YOU'LL NEED

- white cardstock
- red cardstock
- teal cardstock
- cell phone rubber stamp
- 7 small gems
- text rub-on transfer
- white silk flower
- brown ink pad
- scissors or other cutting tool
- ruler
- bone folder (optional)
- glue stick or other adhesive
- craft glue

Long time, no talk? This sassy card will let your friend know you're available any time she's in need of some serious chick-chat.

Cut the white cardstock to 8½" x 5½" (22cm x 14cm). Score and fold to create a card that's 5½" x 4¼" (14cm x 11cm) with the fold at the top of the card. Randomly stamp the cell phone stamp on the front of the card with brown ink.

Trim the red cardstock to 2¼" x 5½" (6cm x 14cm) and glue to the front, approximately ¼" (6mm) from the bottom. Cut the teal cardstock to approximately 1¾" x 4" (4cm x 10cm). Using scissors, make wavy cuts on the short ends.

Glue the teal cardstock left of center on the red cardstock. Glue six of the crystals along the left wavy edge. Apply the rub-on sentiment to the right side of the teal cardstock.

Glue the silk flower to the left of the sentiment, and glue the last crystal to the flower center.

BTW
by the way

CHANGE UP THE BACKGROUND STAMP TO FLOWERS, CUPCAKES, SHOES OR ANYTHING YOU DESIRE. THIS SIMPLE CARD DESIGN OFFERS GREAT FLEXIBILITY FOR ANY OCCASION.

Hi Friend

TERESA WILKINS

WHAT YOU'LL NEED

- orange cardstock
- green cardstock
- black cardstock
- circle-patterned paper
- ABC-patterned paper
- 4½" (11cm) piece of green velvet ribbon
- 6 orange brads
- green chalk pad
- scissors or other cutting tool
- ruler
- bone folder (optional)
- die-cutter with tag and letter dies or pre-cut tags and black letter stickers
- glue stick or other adhesive
- glue dots
- pop dots

Know someone who's feeling funky? A bit sad? A little note to say "hi" will be just enough to brighten her day. Send this card to anyone who needs a little pick-me-up.

Trim the orange cardstock to 8½" x 5½" (22cm x 14cm). Score and fold the cardstock to create a card that is 4¼" x 5½" (11cm x 14cm).

Cut the green cardstock into two pieces measuring 1⅝" x 2" (4cm x 5cm) and one piece measuring 4⅛" x 3¼" (10.4cm x 8.3cm). Tap the edges of all three pieces onto the chalk pad.

Cut the circle-patterned paper to 4" x 3⅛" (10cm x 8cm) and adhere to the cardstock with glue stick.

Cut an *h* and an *i* from the ABC-patterned paper into 1½" x 1⅞" (3.8cm x 4.8cm) pieces and glue to the two small pieces of green cardstock.

Glue the pieces of green cardstock to the front of the card, as shown. Use glue dots to adhere the ribbon to the card below the letters, then trim the ends flush with the card.

Using a die cutter, cut six small tags from the green cardstock and the letters to spell *friend* from black cardstock. Glue each letter onto one of the tags. Attach a brad through the top of each tag, folding both flanges down behind the tag to hide them from view. Arrange the tags diagonally on the circle paper and adhere with pop dots.

Thinking of You

TONIA DAVENPORT

PATTERNED PAPER: KI Memories • PAINTS: Making Memories

Whether your friend has hit a small bump in the road or she's just having a bad week, she'll love hearing that she's in your thoughts.

Trim a piece of watercolor paper to 5⅜" x 7½" (13.7cm x 19cm) and fold to make a 3¾" x 5⅜" (9.5cm x 13.7cm) card. Trim light blue cardstock to 3⅜" x 5" (8.6cm x 12.7cm). Beginning ⅜" (1cm) from the left long side of the blue paper, make six 1" (2.5cm) horizontal cuts at ¾", 1¼", 1½", 2", 2¼" and 2¾" (1.9cm, 3.2cm, 3.8cm, 5cm, 5.7cm and 7cm) from the top, using a ruler, craft knife and cutting mat.

Cut a strip of the striped paper to 5" x ¾" (12.7cm x 1.9cm). Thread the strip through the slits cut in the blue paper and adhere with glue stick. Center the blue paper on the front of the card and adhere with glue stick.

Use a black fine-point pen to draw dashed "stitch" lines around the edge of the blue paper and down either side of the striped paper. Also, include stitches over the blue slits, as shown. Using the same pen, draw a loose flower and a leaf.

Use pink paint and a paintbrush to color in the petals of the flower, and green paint to color in the leaf and flower center, and to make rough stripes across the slits. When the paint is dry, write *thinking of you* along the flower's leaf.

Simply "Hi"

KRISTEN SWAIN

WHAT YOU'LL NEED

- black cardstock
- red cardstock
- friendship-patterned paper
- red flowered paper
- large alphabet stamps
- 3" (8cm) piece of orange ribbon with white dots
- pink and cream fabric flower sticker
- 3 small orange paper flowers
- black ink pad
- black acrylic paint
- scissors or other cutting tool
- ruler
- bone folder (optional)
- stapler with black staples
- 1¼" (3.2cm) sun paper punch
- 2" (5cm) circle punch or template
- 3" (7.6cm) circle punch or template
- glue stick or other adhesive

This unusually pretty card is unusually shaped as well. It's designed like a matchbook, with a little flap at the bottom. What a great design to add to your card repertoire!

Cut the black cardstock to 10¾" x 5" (27cm x 13cm). With the piece horizontal on your table, measure 5" (13cm) from the left edge and score. Make another score line ½" (1.3cm) from the right edge. Fold the card toward the center at each score line.

To keep the small tab up, staple about seven black staples along the folded edge, placing them ⅛" (3mm) from the fold.

Cut a 4½" (11cm) square from the red flowered paper. Using the punches or templates, cut two small circles and one larger circle from the friendship paper, and ink the edges with black ink. Glue the smaller circles behind the large one, letting the smaller circles run off the edge of the flowered paper. Trim the circles flush with the flowered paper. Ink the edges of the flowered paper with black ink.

Glue the flowered paper onto the red cardstock. Trim the cardstock, leaving a ⅛" (3mm) border. Position the black cardstock so that the flap is at the bottom of the card. Glue the layered square onto the black cardstock.

Punch a sun shape from red cardstock. Glue the sun to the center of the fabric flower. Tie a knot in the center of the ribbon, then glue it to the center of the sun. Glue the orange flowers around the knot in the ribbon.

Stamp the greeting on the bottom left of the card with black paint using the large letter stamps.

Smile

STACEY STAMITOLES

WHAT YOU'LL NEED

- lime green cardstock
- bright orange cardstock
- mod stars patterned paper
- mod stripes patterned paper
- text rub-on transfer
- flowers rub-on transfer
- dots rub-on transfer
- 3 paper flowers
- 3 silver brads
- small white tag
- silver square paper clip
- scissors or other cutting tool
- ruler
- bone folder (optional)
- glue stick or other adhesive
- glue dots

Have a friend with a frown?
Who could resist smiling when she receives this card?

Cut the green cardstock to 8½" x 5½" (22cm x 14cm). Score and fold the center to make a card that's 5½" x 4½" (14cm x 11cm) with the fold at the top. Cut the star patterned paper to 5¼" x 4" (13cm x 10cm) and glue to the front of the card.

Cut a piece of green cardstock to 3" x 2¼" (8cm x 6cm) and a piece of orange cardstock to 2" x 2¼" (5cm x 6cm). Apply the rub-on sentiment to the green card and apply rub-on flowers to both cards.

Cut a piece of green cardstock to 5½" x 1¼" (22cm x 3.2cm). Cut a piece of striped paper to 5½" x 1" (22cm x 2.5cm) and glue to the center of the green strip. Insert a brad into the center of each paper flower and attach to the strip.

Apply glue to just the short ends of the paper strip and glue it to the front of the card. Insert the green and orange cardstock pieces behind the strip and glue into place. Apply rub-on dots to the white tag, then attach the tag to the card with the square paper clip.

Call Me

LINDA BEESON

WHAT YOU'LL NEED

- striped/lime green double-sided cardstock
- green cardstock
- red cardstock
- turquoise paper
- circle-patterned paper
- telephone sticker
- red snap
- assorted rub-on transfers
- red distress stamp pad
- scissors or other cutting tool
- ruler
- bone folder (optional)
- sewing machine (optional)
- 1¾" (4.5cm) circle template or punch
- 2" (5cm) circle template or punch
- glue stick or other adhesive

A card like this lets your girlfriend know you'd love to hear from her—anytime, anywhere.

Cut a 5½" x 11" (14cm x 28cm) piece from the double-sided striped cardstock. Score the center and fold to create a card that is 5½" (14cm) square, with the stripes on the outside. Ink the edges of the card with the stamp pad.

Cut a 4½" (11cm) square from green cardstock. Center it on the front of the card and glue in place. To make the photo corners, cut two 1" (2.5cm) squares from red cardstock. Cut the squares in half diagonally, then cut a triangle-shaped notch in each half. Glue the photo corners to the corners of the green cardstock. If you like, machine stitch along the edges of each photo corner.

Use a circle template or punch to make a 1¾" (4.5cm) circle from the circle-patterned paper. Cut a 2" (5cm) circle from the turquoise paper and glue the two circles together. Place the telephone sticker on the center of the layered circles, then set a snap above the sticker.

Glue the layered circle onto the card. Use the rub-on transfers to spell out different sentiments on the green cardstock.

Hello Friend

LINDA BEESON

WHITE CARDSTOCK: Bazzill Basics • RED CARDSTOCK: Die Cuts With a View • PATTERNED PAPER: NRN Designs • RIBBON: Offray • ALPHABET STICKERS: Bo-Bunny Press • RUB-ON TRANSFERS: Chatterbox

WHAT YOU'LL NEED

- white cardstock
- red cardstock
- red and pink patterned paper
- 8" (20cm) piece of pink ribbon with white dots
- large alphabet stickers
- small alphabet rub-on transfers
- scissors or other cutting tool
- ruler
- sandpaper
- bone folder (optional)

Haven't called your friend in a while? Let her know you haven't forgotten her with this happy "hello."

Cut the white cardstock to 6½" x 9½" (17cm x 24cm), then score the center to create a card that's 6½" x 4¾" (17cm x 12cm) with the fold at the top.

Cut the patterned paper to 5¾" x 4 1/16" (14.6cm x 10.3cm) and round the edges with the corner rounder or with scissors. Cut a piece of red cardstock to 5 7/8" x 4 3/16" (14.9cm x 10.6cm). Glue the patterned paper to the red cardstock. Round the corners of the cardstock as well. Glue the layered piece to the front of the card.

Cut a 5" x 2½" (13cm x 6cm) piece from the red cardstock, and round the two corners on the right side. Wrap the ribbon around the left side of the red cardstock and tie a knot in the front. Glue the cardstock to the card, aligning it with the left side of the patterned paper.

Lightly sand the letter stickers that spell *Hello*, then adhere them to the center piece of cardstock. Use the small rub-on transfers to spell the word *friend*.

Daisies

JUDI WATANABE

WHAT YOU'LL NEED

- metallic gold cardstock
- white cardstock
- daisy rubber stamp
- 20" (50cm) piece of pink and yellow gingham ribbon
- black permanent ink pad
- yellow and orange colored pencils and markers
- scissors or other cutting tool
- ruler
- bone folder (optional)
- glue stick or other adhesive
- glue dot

CARDSTOCK AND RUBBER STAMP, JudiKins

What could be cheerier than a daisy? A whole card full of them, of course!

Cut the gold cardstock to 8½" x 5½" (22cm x 14cm). Score and fold the center to make a card that's 4½" x 5½" (11cm x 14cm).

Cut the white cardstock to 2½" x 5½" (6cm x 14cm). Stamp the daisy onto the white cardstock with black ink, overlapping some of the petals and running some of the daisies off the edges of the cardstock. Color the centers of the daisies with yellow and orange markers and colored pencils.

Glue the stamped cardstock to the center of the card. Cut the ribbon to 11" (28cm) and wrap it around the left side of the card, near the fold, gluing the ends on the inside of the card. Tie the remaining ribbon into a bow and adhere it to the center of the ribbon with a glue dot.

BTW by the way

NOT SURE WHEN TO USE WHICH KIND OF INK? CHECK OUT PAGE 85 FOR SOME HELPFUL TIPS.

Ponytail Day
JUDI WATANABE

WHAT YOU'LL NEED

- olive green cardstock
- cream cardstock
- white paper
- solid dots rubber stamp cube
- floral paisley rubber stamp
- metallic purple string
- coordinating ponytail holder
- dusty blue ink pad
- sage green ink pad
- tan ink pad
- orange ink pad
- yellow ink pad
- plum ink pad
- mini envelope template
- scissors or other cutting tool
- ruler
- bone folder (optional)
- glue stick or other adhesive
- font: American Typewriter

For those days that are literally "bad hair" days, send this card that reads: "Some days it's just a ponytail kind of day."

Cut a piece of olive green cardstock to 7½" x 8½" (19cm x 22cm). Score and fold the center to create a card that's 3¾" x 8½" (9.5cm x 22cm).

Stamp a sheet of white paper for the envelope, beginning with the largest dot and the dusty blue ink. Continue stamping smaller dots with the other colored inks, progressing from green and tan to orange and yellow. Finally, stamp the floral paisleys with plum ink over the entire sheet of paper.

Trace the mini envelope pattern onto the stamped paper, cut out and assemble. To line the envelope flap, copy the "flap" section of the template onto another sheet of white

paper. Cut it out, extending the bottom edge 1" to 2" (2.5cm to 5cm). Glue the lining onto just the inside flap, with the extra length inside the envelope.

Use the center of the envelope template to make a square card with the cream cardstock. Print the sentiment *Sometimes it's just a ponytail kind of day* on white paper. Cut out around the text and ink the paper lightly with the orange and yellow ink pads. Glue this to the cardstock square. Tie the coordinating ponytail holder to the card with metallic string.

Slip the card inside the envelope and glue the envelope to the front of the tall card.

The Going Gets Tough

ANABELLE O'MALLEY

CARDSTOCK, PATTERNED PAPER AND RUBBER STAMPS: Paper Salon • BRADS: Making Memories • FONT: Two Peas in a Bucket

WHAT YOU'LL NEED

- pink cardstock
- light blue cardstock
- white cardstock
- brown cardstock
- striped paper
- paisley-patterned paper
- paisley rubber stamp
- bon bons rubber stamp
- 5½" piece of white trim
- 2 white brads
- pink ink pad
- brown ink pad
- colored pencils
- scissors or other cutting tool
- ruler
- bone folder (optional)
- scalloped decorative scissors
- corner rounder (optional)
- glue stick or other adhesive
- craft glue
- font: AL Anytime

Everyone has rough days, and what better way to lift a friend's spirits than with chocolates? Let her know she deserves a bit of chocolate today and every day.

Cut the pink cardstock to 8½" x 5½" (22cm x 14cm). Score and fold to create a card that's 5½" x 4¼" (14cm x 11cm) with the fold at the top of the card. Using the pink ink pad, stamp the paisley design randomly over the entire card.

Print the text on light blue cardstock. Trim the cardstock to 5½" x ⅝" (14cm x 16mm) and glue it to the card, about ¼" (6mm) from the bottom.

Cut a piece of striped paper to 5½" x ½" (14cm x 1.3cm). Cut two pieces of paisley paper to 5½" x ³⁄₁₆" (14cm x 5mm), cutting one long edge of each paisley piece with the scalloped scissors.

Insert brads into the striped paper, placing one approximately 1¾" (4.5cm) in from each end. Glue the striped paper and one of the paisley strips to the center of the card so that the scalloped strip shows below the striped one.

Adhere the white trim along the top of the card with craft glue, then glue the second strip of paisley paper over the trim so that the top edge is flush with the fold.

Stamp the bon bons image with brown ink onto white cardstock. Trim the image to 1⅛" x 2⅛" (2.9cm x 5.4cm). Round the corners with a corner rounder or scissors, and color the image with colored pencils. Glue the stamped image onto brown cardstock and trim, leaving a narrow border of brown. Glue onto the center of the card between the two brads.

Cheer Up
CINDY CURTIS

WHAT YOU'LL NEED

- black cardstock
- tropical-patterned paper
- letter stickers
- pink silk flower
- white paint pen
- gem
- scissors or other cutting tool
- ruler
- craft knife
- cutting mat
- bone folder (optional)
- glue stick or other adhesive
- craft glue

Cheering someone up can be no easy task. But this playful card is sure to help.

Cut the black cardstock to 8" x 7½" (20cm x 19cm). Score and fold to create a card that's 3¾" x 8" (95mm x 20cm). Cut out a square from the front of the card, that's 1" (2.5cm) from the top and centered side to side.

Trim the drinks portion of the tropical paper into a square that measures 2⅜" (6cm). Glue the paper to the inside of the card, so that it shows through the window on the front.

Use the white marker to make dots around the edge of the window. Adhere the flower to the upper-right corner of the window and a gem to the center of the flower with craft glue.

Place the letter stickers below the window, and dress them up with more white dots.

BTW
→ by the way ↔

HAVEN'T CUT A WINDOW IN A CARD BEFORE? OPEN YOUR CARD FLAT ON A CUTTING MAT. LIGHTLY DRAW THE SHAPE YOU WANT TO CUT OUT ON THE FRONT OF THE CARD. USE A RULER AND CRAFT KNIFE TO CUT SLIGHTLY OUTSIDE YOUR MARKS SO YOU DON'T NEED TO WORRY ABOUT ERASING YOUR GUIDELINES.

Ab Fab

CHRISTINE DOYLE

WHAT YOU'LL NEED

- black cardstock
- red cardstock
- martini-patterned paper
- text rub-on transfer
- scissors or other cutting tool
- craft knife
- cutting mat
- ruler
- bone folder (optional)
- glue stick or other adhesive

CARDSTOCK: Bazzill Basics • PATTERNED PAPER: Zsiage • RUB-ON TRANSFER: Making Memories

No matter how she's feeling about herself, let her know you think she's always absolutely fabulous with this card.

Cut the black cardstock to 8" x 4½" (20cm x 11cm). Score the center and fold to make a card that's 4" x 4½" (10cm x 11cm).

Trim a 4" (10cm) square around the martini glass on the patterned paper. Glue the square to the front of the card, placing it ¼" (6mm) from the fold. Using scissors and a craft knife and cutting mat, trim approximately ⅞" (2.2cm) of paper away from the right side of the martini glass, cutting around the glass but flush with the edge of the card.

Cut a piece of red cardstock to 4" x 4½" (10cm x 11cm) and glue to the inside of the card. Rub on the sentiment to the left of the glass.

Glam It Up!

Do you have a fashion queen in your group of friends? The girl who always looks put together? The one with the most fabulous shoes and handbags? These cards are for her—and for all those fashion-queen wannabes out there. Whether your friend favors vintage clothes or simply every kind of shoe, there's a card here for her.

Red Dress

ANNA ARMENDARIZ

WHAT YOU'LL NEED

- red cardstock
- circle-patterned paper
- red button
- black pen
- scissors
- ruler
- bone folder (optional)
- glue stick or other adhesive
- craft glue

Every woman loves to feel sexy. And what's sexier than a little red dress? Celebrate all things feminine with this flirty little number.

Fold a 8½" x 5½" (22cm x 14cm) piece of red cardstock in half, then freehand cut the shape of a dress. It's not necessary to have part of the dress on the fold. Place glue on the ends of the dress straps and glue the front of the card to the back.

Cut a sash for the dress about ⅜" (9mm) wide from the patterned paper, and cut two smaller pieces for the ends of the sash. Glue all three pieces onto the dress, then adhere the button onto the sash with craft glue to cover the ends of the two smaller pieces.

Outline the dress with a random dashed line using the black pen. Handwrite the following quote on the hemline: *"When in doubt ... wear red."*—Bill Blass

For the ruffle at the bottom of the dress, cut a piece of red cardstock to 5" x 1¼" (13cm x 3cm). Accordion fold the cardstock, starting at one short end, making folds that are about ½" (1.3cm) wide. Unfold the paper and glue to the bottom inside front of the card. Trim to match the edges of the dress, leaving a ⅛" (3mm) ruffle below the hem of the dress.

BTW
by the way

WHEN OUTLINING THE EDGE OF THE CARD, DON'T WORRY ABOUT BEING PERFECT! LEAVING SOME OF THE LINES UNCONNECTED OR A LITTLE CROOKED ADDS TO THE PLAYFULNESS OF THE CARD. JUST HAVE FUN!

Special Purse-On Card

ANABELLE O'MALLEY

WHAT YOU'LL NEED

- light blue cardstock
- white cardstock
- red cardstock
- squares-patterned paper
- vellum paper
- purse rubber stamp
- black ink pad
- light blue ink pad
- blue, green and red markers and colored pencils
- scissors or other cutting tool
- ruler
- bone folder (optional)
- 2½" (6.4cm) scallop circle punch
- 1¾" (4.5cm) circle punch
- small sponge
- glue stick or other adhesive
- font: Fancy Free

This little notecard will brighten up any girlfriend's day—especially if she loves purses! Send it to let her know you're thinking of her, to thank her for a gift, or just to say "hello."

Cut the light blue cardstock to 8½" x 5½" (22cm x 14cm). Score and fold to create a card that's 4¼" x 5½" (11cm x 14cm). Cut the patterned paper to 4" x 5¼" (10cm x 13cm), and glue to the front of the card.

Print the text onto vellum paper, leaving a space in the center for the purse image, and trim the paper to 1¾" x 5¼" (45mm x 10cm). Place glue on the center of the strip only and stick on the center of the card.

Punch a scalloped circle from the red cardstock, then glue it to the center of the vellum strip, covering the glue you used to glue the vellum to the patterned paper.

Punch a circle from white cardstock. Stamp the purse in the center of the circle with black ink. Color the purse in with markers and colored pencils. Tap the dry sponge on the light blue inkpad and sponge around the edge of the circle. When it's dry, glue the purse circle to the center of the scalloped circle.

BTW by the way

OTHER SENTIMENTS THAT WOULD GO GREAT WITH THIS CARD INCLUDE: *YOU'VE GOT PURSE-ONALITY AND PURSE-ONALLY, I THINK YOU'RE THE BEST.* HAVE "PUN" WITH IT!

In Fine Form

SHERRY WRIGHT

CARDSTOCK, PATTERNED PAPER AND RUBBER STAMPS: Paper Salon • FLOWERS: Prima • LACE: Fibers By The Yard • RHINESTONES: Swarovski

WHAT YOU'LL NEED

- pink cardstock
- white cardstock
- paisley-patterned paper
- dress form rubber stamp
- text rubber stamp
- 14" (36m) piece of lace, ¾" (1.9cm) wide
- 20 gems
- 4 silk flowers in shades of pink
- brown ink pad
- colored pencils
- scissors or other cutting tool
- ruler
- bone folder (optional)
- 3" x 4" (8cm x 10cm) oval cutter or template
- BeJeweler tool
- glue stick or other adhesive
- craft glue

This girly dress form sets just the right tone for a card fit for your most fashionable friends. And the sparkles help too.

Cut the pink cardstock to 8½" x 5½" (22cm x 14cm). Score and fold to create a card that's 4¼" x 5½" (11cm x 14cm). Cut a piece of paisley paper to 3" x 5¼" (8cm x 13cm) and ink the edges with brown ink.

Cut the lace into two pieces that are 7" (18cm) each. Place the lace on the long sides of the card, about ⅛" (3mm) in from the edge. Glue the ends of the lace onto the back of the front cover of the card to secure.

Cut a 3" x 4" (8cm x 10cm) oval from white cardstock. Stamp the dress form in the center of the oval with brown ink, then stamp the text alongside the dress form. Color the stamp with colored pencils.

Glue the oval to the upper center of the paisley paper, then glue the paisley paper over the lace on the center of the card.

Heat up the BeJeweler tool and glue sixteen rhinestones around the edge of the oval, spacing them somewhat equally. Draw dashes between the rhinestones with brown colored pencil.

Glue one flower to the top left of the oval and cluster three more below the oval at the right. Glue the remaining rhinestones to the centers of the flowers.

Twirl
CHRISTINE DOYLE

WHAT YOU'LL NEED

- blue cardstock
- white cardstock
- flowered paper
- dress rubber stamp
- 20" (51cm) piece of narrow green satin ribbon
- 2 coordinating beads
- sage green ink pad
- yellow gel crayon or pastel
- blue colored pencil
- scissors or other cutting tool
- ruler
- bone folder (optional)
- makeup applicator (optional)
- needle (optional)
- glue stick or other adhesive

Know someone who just has to twirl each time she puts on a pretty dress? While this card doesn't actually say "twirl," it's a great word to add to any card that has a fun, feminine feel.

Cut the blue cardstock to 8½" x 5½" (22cm x 14cm). Score and fold the center to make a card that's 4¼" x 5½" (11cm x 14cm). Cut the flowered paper to 4" x 5¼" (10cm x 13cm) and glue to the front of the card.

Cut the white cardstock to 2⅜" x 3¼" (6.7cm x 8.3cm). Stamp the dress image in the center with the green ink pad. Ink the edges of the cardstock as well. Color the dress with the gel crayon or pastel, using your finger or a makeup applicator to get a nice soft color. Color the sash with a blue colored pencil.

Glue the white cardstock to the flowered paper, placing it a little higher than center.

Thread a bead onto each end of the ribbon, simply by pushing the ribbon through the hole in the bead or using a needle. Tie a double knot below each bead to keep it from sliding off the ribbon. Tie the ribbon on the fold of the card, making sure that one bead is higher than the other. Trim the ends of the ribbon at an angle.

It's a Girl Thing

NICOLE JACKSON

CARDSTOCK AND RUBBER STAMP: Paper Salon • FLOWERS: Prima

WHAT YOU'LL NEED

- white cardstock
- dot-patterned paper
- shoe and text rubber stamp
- 3" (7.6cm) pieces of various ribbons and trims
- 12" (30cm) piece of trim for border
- 6" (15cm) piece of $7/8$" (2.2cm)-wide black velvet ribbon
- 7 small mulberry flowers
- black ink pad
- watercolor pencils
- scissors or other cutting tool
- ruler
- bone folder (optional)
- stapler
- glue dots
- 1" (2.5cm) glue tape

Know a girl who loves dressing up, fine shoes, and pretty trim? Share your love of ribbon with her by sending this tailored card.

Cut the white cardstock to 8½" x 5½" (22cm x 14cm). Score and fold to create a card that's 4¼" x 5½" (11cm x 14cm). Hand cut a curve along the edge opposite the fold on the front cover.

Fold the small pieces of ribbon in half and staple them to the curve, keeping the staples close to the curve and the folds aligned with the back panel of the card. With scissors, trim any ribbon ends that extend past the staple.

Using glue tape, adhere the long piece of trim to the card along the curve, covering the staples. Adhere the trim to both the front and back of the curve. Using glue dots, glue the small flowers along the trim, placing one by each piece of ribbon.

Stamp the shoe and text on white cardstock with black ink. Color the image with watercolor pencils, as desired, then trim to 1¼" x 1¾" (3.2cm x 4.5cm). Glue the image onto the dot-patterned paper, centering it inside a frame of dots, and trim to 2" x 2½" (5cm x 6.4cm).

Use the glue tape to glue the velvet ribbon to the front of the card and trim any excess from the ends. Glue the trimmed dotted paper to the center of the velvet ribbon.

Feeling Groovy

JUDI WATANABE

WHAT YOU'LL NEED

- black glossy cardstock
- white cardstock
- solid boomerang rubber stamp
- solid triangle rubber stamp
- retro dancers rubber stamp
- retro stars rubber stamp
- hot pink ink pad
- lime green ink pad
- yellow ink pad
- orange ink pad
- black pigment ink pad
- gray ink pad
- black or clear embossing powder
- scissors or other cutting tool
- ruler
- bone folder (optional)
- heat gun
- glue stick or other adhesive

Pay tribute to a groovy chick with this colorful card. Swing it, baby!

CARDSTOCK AND RUBBER STAMPS: Judikins

Cut the black cardstock to 8½" x 5½" (22cm x 14cm). Score and fold to create a card that's 5½" x 4¼" (14cm x 11cm) with the fold at the top.

Cut the white cardstock to 4" x 6" (10cm x 15cm). Stamp the boomerang and triangle shapes with hot pink, lime green, yellow and orange ink. Overlap the shapes and run them off the edge of the paper. Let the inks dry completely.

Stamp the dancers in black ink across the center of the card and heat emboss with black or clear embossing powder. Stamp the retro stars with the gray ink.

Trim the white cardstock to 5½" x 3¼" (14cm x 11cm), making sure that the dancers are centered top to bottom. Glue the image to the center of the folded card.

BTW *by the way*

HEAT EMBOSSING GIVES A GLOSSY, DIMENSIONAL LOOK TO A STAMPED IMAGE. FIRST STAMP THE IMAGE WITH PIGMENT INK. SPRINKLE EMBOSSING POWDER OVER THE WET INK AND TAP OFF THE EXCESS. THEN HEAT THE POWDER WITH A HEAT GUN UNTIL IT MELTS. IT'S THAT EASY!

Never Too Many

KELLY ANNE GRUNDHAUSER

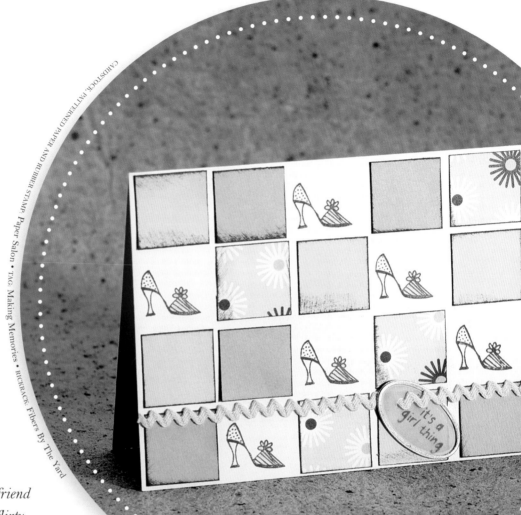

WHAT YOU'LL NEED

- white cardstock
- pink cardstock
- green cardstock
- flowered paper
- shoe and text rubber stamp
- oval vellum tag
- 6" (15cm) piece of pink rickrack
- brown ink pad
- pink marker
- scissors or other cutting tool
- ruler
- bone folder (optional)
- glue stick or other adhesive
- craft glue

Who doesn't have at least one friend with a passion for shoes? The flirty colors and fabulous shoe stamp make this card a real kick.

Cut the white cardstock to 8½" x 5½" (22cm x 14cm). Score and fold to create a card that's 5½" x 4¼" (14cm x 11cm) with the fold on top.

Cut five 1" (2.5cm) squares from each of the pink and green cardstocks and four from the flowered paper. Ink the edges of each square with brown ink. Glue the squares to the front of the card, leaving ⅛" (3mm) of space between each square. Leave six square openings for the shoe stamp.

Stamp the shoe in each of the six empty squares, using brown ink. Color the toe of each shoe with the marker.

Stamp the text in brown ink onto the vellum tag. Slide the tag onto the length of rickrack. With craft glue, adhere the rickrack across the top of the bottom row of squares, letting the tag hang. Trim the ends of the rickrack flush with the edges of the card.

BTW
→ *by the way*

A SIMPLE DESIGN LIKE THIS ONE IS EASY TO CHANGE UP FOR VARIETY. PUT THE RECIPIENT'S INITIALS ON THE TAG OR USE A FLOWER OR PURSE STAMP INSTEAD OF THE SHOE.

If The Shoe Fits

MIKI BENEDICT

CARDSTOCK, PATTERNED PAPERS AND RUBBER STAMP: Paper Salon • RIBBON: Fibers By The Yard

WHAT YOU'LL NEED

- light blue cardstock
- brown cardstock
- green cardstock
- pink cardstock
- paisley-patterned paper
- striped paper
- shoe stamp
- 8" (20cm) piece of of sheer pink ribbon with white dots
- 8" (20cm) piece of sheer brown ribbon with white dots
- brown ink pad
- scissors or other cutting tool
- ruler
- bone folder (optional)
- glue stick or other adhesive
- craft glue
- font: A Yummy Apology

Love your girlfriends … support their shopping habits! Using coordinating colors and patterns, you can put this card together in a snap.

Cut the light blue cardstock to 8½" x 5½" (22cm x 14cm). Score and fold to create a card that's 4¼" x 5½" (11cm x 14cm). Cut the brown cardstock to 4" x 5¼" (10cm x 13cm), and ink the edges with the brown ink pad.

Print the text on green cardstock, then trim the paper to a 1¾" (4.5cm) square. Cut a piece of pink cardstock to the same size and stamp the shoe in the center with brown ink. Cut one 1¼" (3.2cm) square from each of the patterned papers.

Ink the edges of all the squares with brown ink. Glue the squares to the brown cardstock as shown.

Cut 3" (7.6cm) from one end of each of ribbon. Loosely tie the small pieces to the large pieces of ribbon, placing the knot approximately ¾" (1.9cm) from one end. Place the pink ribbon across the brown cardstock, wrapping the ends around the back and securing them with craft glue. Repeat with the brown ribbon, placing it below the pink one.

BTW
by the way

IF YOU HAVE A STASH OF SQUARE PAPER PUNCHES, USE THOSE TO CUT THE SQUARES FOR THIS CARD.

So Chic
LINDA BEESON

CARDSTOCK, PATTERNED PAPER AND RUBBER STAMPS: Paper Salon • BRADS: Karen Foster

WHAT YOU'LL NEED

- pink cardstock
- brown cardstock
- light blue cardstock
- paisley-patterned paper
- flower rubber stamp
- text rubber stamp
- brown ink pad
- 1" (2.5cm) circle punch
- 3 white brads
- scissors or other cutting tool
- ruler
- bone folder (optional)
- glue stick or other adhesive

This sooo chic greeting is just plain fun.
And punching the circles makes it fast, fast, fast!

Cut the pink cardstock to 8½" x 5½" (22cm x 14cm). Score and fold to create a card that's 5½" x 4¼" (14cm x 11cm) with the fold at the top. Ink the edges of the card with brown ink.

Punch four circles from each of the brown and blue cardstocks and from the patterned paper. Ink the edges of all the circles with brown ink.

Stamp the three flowers on pink cardstock with brown ink. Trim around the flowers, leaving a thin border of pink around each petal. Use the brown ink to stamp the text onto one of the blue circles.

Glue the pink flowers onto the remaining blue circles. Insert a brad into the center of each. Glue all the circles to the front of the card in a grid pattern, as shown.

All Laced Up

KELLY ANNE GRUNDHAUSER

WHAT YOU'LL NEED

- green cardstock
- white cardstock
- striped paper
- lady-with-packages rubber stamp
- 6" (15cm) piece of sheer blue ribbon with white dots
- 6 brads with loops for lacing
- text rub-on transfer
- light green ink pad
- light blue ink pad
- black ink pad
- colored pencils
- scissors or other cutting tool
- ruler
- bone folder (optional)
- glue stick or other adhesive
- glitter glue in green, blue and lavender

The sense of anticipation your friend gets from unlacing this card makes whatever there is inside all the more memorable. If you have a friend who's patience-impaired, glue or sew the bottom of the card and use it as a pocket.

Cut a piece of green cardstock to 8½" x 5½" (22cm x 14cm). With the cardstock horizontal on your work surface, measure 1½" (3.8cm) from the left edge and score on this line. Measure 2¾" (7cm) from the right edge and score. Fold both edges toward the center of the card to form a gatefold in the front.

Cut the striped paper to 5½" x 4¼" (14cm x 11cm) and glue it to the inside of the card. Cut another piece to 1" x 5½" (2.5cm x 14cm) and glue slightly right of center on the right panel of the front of the card. Ink all edges of the card with light green and light blue inks.

With black ink, stamp the lady shopper image onto white cardstock. Trim to 2⅛" x 1⅞" (5.4cm x 4.8cm), then ink the edges of the paper with black ink. Color in the image with colored pencils and add detail with glitter glue. Glue the image to the front of the card, about ½" (1.3cm) from the top edge, centered on the striped paper.

For the placement of the brads, measure ½", 1¼" and 2" (1.3cm, 3.2cm and 5cm) up from the bottom and ½" (1.3cm) from the edge of each panel, making marks at each of these points with a pencil. Insert a brad at each mark.

Lace the ribbon through the brads, starting at the bottom and tying at the top. Embellish the brads with more glitter glue if you like.

Apply the rub-on transfer to the left side of the card.

Vintage Girl

JEANETTE BESHEARS

PLAID AND GREEN PATTERNED PAPERS, Daisy's D's • DOTTED PAPER, Making Memories • STRIPED RIBBON, Go With the Grain • DARK PINK RIBBON: Offray • EARRING, Jewelry & Handbag Warehouse • WIRED BEADS AND ACRYLIC FLOWER, Hirschberg Schultz & Co. • CLEAR GEM: Westrim • PLAID AND GREEN AND WHITE CARDSTOCK: The Paper Company • LEAF GREEN AND WHITE CARDSTOCK: Canson • PINK CARDSTOCK: Canson

WHAT YOU'LL NEED

- dark pink cardstock
- leaf green cardstock
- white cardstock
- plaid paper
- green patterned paper
- pink paper with white dots
- pink-and-green striped ribbon
- dark pink ribbon
- white thread
- pink rhinestone earring
- wired beads
- small pink acrylic flower

- small clear acrylic gem
- scissors
- ruler
- paper trimmer (optional)
- bone folder (optional)
- scalloped-edge scissors
- corner rounder (optional)
- wire cutters

- glue stick
- double-sided tape
- jewelry glue or craft glue
- foam mounting tape
- patterns on page 91

Everything old is new again! This card has vintage charm from its plaid wrap dress to the rhinestone jewelry. Whether your friend prefers hunting through thrift stores or the mall, she'll love this card.

Dear Danielle,

I saw this cute, little vintage clothing shop at Fourth and Main and thought of you. It's just your style. Let's check it out soon!

Love,
Jeanette

SEND THIS AS A BIRTHDAY CARD, AND USE THE OTHER EARRING TO MAKE A CHOKER NECKLACE AS A GIFT.

Cut the dark pink cardstock to 9½" x 6¾" (24cm x 17cm). Score and fold the center to create a card that's 4¾" x 6¾" (12cm x 17cm). Cut the leaf green cardstock to 4½" x 6½" (11.5cm x 16.5cm) and the plaid paper to 4¼" x 6¼" (10.8cm x 15.9cm). Glue the plaid paper to the center of the green cardstock.

Cut a strip of leaf green cardstock to 1½" x 6½" (3.8cm x 16.5cm), then use the scalloped-edge scissors to trim approximately ¼" (6mm) from the long sides of the strip. Cut the striped ribbon to 8" (20cm). Tie a thread in the center of the ribbon to gather it a bit. Use double-sided tape to adhere the ribbon to the strip of green cardstock. Tape the green strip approximately ¼" (6mm) from the bottom edge of the plaid paper. Tape the excess ribbon to the back of the layered piece, then tape the layered piece to the pink card. Cut off the back of the earring with wire cutters, and attach it to the gathered part of the ribbon with jewelry glue or craft glue.

Make a copy of the patterns on page 91. Placing the front of the patterns so that they touch the back of the patterned paper, trace and cut the partial skirt from both the green patterned and pink dotted papers. Tape the green partial skirt over the pink partial skirt, leaving a narrow border of pink showing along the right edge.

Cut the full skirt and the two pieces of the bodice from green patterned paper. Cut the armholes and the skirt trim from the dotted paper. Tape the trim to the skirt pieces and the sleeves of the blouse. Tape the partial skirt on the right side of the full skirt. Tape the bodice to the top of the skirt.

Tape the dark pink ribbon to the neckline and across the waist of the dress, leaving about 4" (10cm) of ribbon hanging from the waist and left neckline; tie these strands of ribbon into a bow.

Tape the completed dress to white cardstock and trim, leaving a ⅛" (3mm) border around the dress. Tape the dress to the front of the card.

Cut the purse pieces from the dotted paper. Tape the pieces to white cardstock and trim, leaving a narrow border. Tape the flap to the purse, then use jewelry glue or craft glue to attach the strung beads to the purse for a handle. Glue the flower to the flap of the purse and the gem to the center of the flower. Attach the purse to the card with foam tape.

To decorate the inside of the card as shown here, cut another piece of leaf green cardstock to 4½" x 6½" (11.5cm x 16.5cm) and the plaid paper to 4¼" x 6¼" (10.8cm x 15.9cm). Glue the plaid paper to the center of the green cardstock and then glue this to the inside of the card.

Cut another scalloped piece from the green cardstock, making it 6½" (16.5cm) long. Cut a piece of pink cardstock to 1⅞" x 6½" (4.8cm x 16.5cm) and glue it to the center of the scalloped piece. Cut the striped ribbon to 6½" (16.5cm) and notch each end with scissors. Use double-sided tape to adhere this to the pink strip, and then adhere the whole strip to the center of the inside of the card.

Print your sentiment onto white cardstock. Trim it to a 2¼" x 3½" (5.7cm x 9cm) rectangle and round the corners. Layer this onto a piece of green cardstock cut to 2¾" x 4" (7cm x 10cm). Center this piece over the ribbon and glue in place.

Where to Shop
STACEY STAMITOLES

This bright card with its sassy sentiment is sure to bring a smile— and probably the urge to hit a favorite boutique.

Cut the green cardstock to 5" x 10" (13cm x 26cm). Score and fold the center to create a 5" (13cm) square card with the fold at the top. Cut a piece of black cardstock to 4½" (11.4cm) square and glue to the center of the front of the card. Cut the striped paper to 4¼" (11cm) square and glue to the center of the black cardstock.

Trim the chipboard to 1¼" x 1½" (3.2cm x 3.8cm). Cut two pieces of ribbon to 2" (5cm). Glue both ends of one piece to the front of the chipboard, like a handle. Do the same on the back of the piece of chipboard with the second piece of ribbon. Glue the flowered paper to the front of the chipboard, covering the ribbon ends.

Glue a paper flower on the purse and dab the center with glitter glue. Ink the bottom and side edges of the purse with the pink ink pad.

Cut a piece of black cardstock to 5" x ⁹⁄₁₆" (13cm x 1.4cm) and glue it just above the bottom of the striped paper. Glue paper flowers onto the strip, then dab glitter glue onto the flower centers. Set aside to allow the glitter glue to dry.

Using a word-processing program, create a text box and type your sentiment into the box. Add a striped border around the box if you like. Print the text box on green cardstock. Trim around the box, then glue it onto a piece of black cardstock. Trim the black cardstock to leave a ⅛" (3mm) border.

Glue the text to the top left of the card with glue stick. Adhere the purse to the lower right of the card with foam tape.

Glamour
CHRISTINE DOYLE

PATTERNED PAPER: MOD • RUBBER STAMP: My Sentiments Exactly! • FLOWER BRAD: Making Memories

- black cardstock
- green paper
- flowered paper
- dress rubber stamp
- clear flower brad
- green ink pad
- black fine-tip pen
- color duster or stippling brush
- ruler
- scissors
- bone folder (optional)
- craft knife
- cutting mat
- glue stick or other adhesive

Some scrapbook paper patterns are just so beautiful they should be printed on fabric so that we can all have dresses made out of them. Until that happens, make do by creating beautiful greeting-card dresses to share.

Cut the black cardstock to 8½" x 5¼" (22cm x 13cm). Score and fold the center to create a card that's 4¼" x 5¼" (11cm x 13cm).

Cut the green paper to 3⅞" x 5" (10cm x 13cm). Tap the color duster (or a stiff-bristled paintbrush, such as a stippling brush) onto the green ink pad. Pounce the color onto the green paper, adding more in the corners.

Stamp the dress stamp in green ink on the backside of the flowered paper. Use the stamp as a pattern to cut out the shape of the dress. Glue the dress to the center of the green paper.

Trace around the dress shape with the black pen, then use the pen to make a border ⅛" (3mm) in from the edges of the green paper. Write *glamour* with the black pen as well.

Make a small slit at the center of the waist of the dress. Insert the flower brad flanges through the slit and spread to secure the brad. Glue the green paper to the center of the card.

BTW
▹ by the way ◃

ADDING COLOR TO PAPER USING AN INK PAD AND COLOR DUSTER TAKES A WHILE. BUT BECAUSE THE PROCESS IS GRADUAL, YOU HAVE MORE CONTROL OVER HOW MUCH COLOR GOES WHERE AND THE LOOK IS SOFTER THAN WIPING THE INK PAD DIRECTLY ON THE PAPER.

happy 29th (again)

you are my favorite Mom

It's All About You

Every girlfriend deserves a
special day, whether it's her
bridal shower, birthday or just
a girls' night out in her honor.
The cards in this section will
make her feel like the princess
at her very own ball—or
at least make her laugh
when you wish her a
happy 29th. . .again.

To You

LINDA BEESON

WHAT YOU'LL NEED

- purple cardstock
- yellow cardstock
- mosaic-patterned paper
- circle-patterned paper
- dot-patterned paper
- text rub-on transfers
- red paper flower
- purple brad
- brown ink pad
- sewing machine with red thread
- monogram template
- scissors or other cutting tool
- ruler
- bone folder (optional)
- glue stick or other adhesive
- foam mounting tape

Your message of cheer will come through loud and clear with this bold and beautiful greeting card.

Cut the purple cardstock to 5½" x 11" (14cm x 28cm). Score and fold the center to create a card that's 5½" (14cm) square. Cut the mosaic-patterned paper to 5¼" x 10¾" (13.3cm x 27.3cm). Glue it to the inside of the card.

Cut the light yellow cardstock to 5¼" (13.3cm) square. Cut a 5" (12.7cm) square from the circle-patterned paper, then ink the edges with the brown ink pad.

Cut a 3" x 5" (7.6cm x 12.7cm) strip from the dotted paper and use scissors to round one of the long sides. Sew this to the circle-patterned paper with a zigzag stitch. Glue this piece to the yellow cardstock, and glue this onto the front of the card. Use rub-on transfers to spell *To You* on the front.

Using the monogram template, cut an *H* and a *B* from the dotted paper. Ink the edges of the letters with the brown ink pad. Glue the letters to the purple cardstock and trim, leaving a ⅛" (3mm) border. Ink the edges of the cardstock. Attach the red flower to the lower-right side of the letter B, using the brad as the center of the flower. Adhere the letters to the inside of the card with foam tape. Use rub-on transfers to spell *happy birthday* on the inside of the card.

Happy Birthday to You

CINDY CURTIS

WHAT YOU'LL NEED

- black cardstock
- striped paper
- "happy birthday" music-patterned paper
- 5 small silk flowers
- 5-6 gems with flat backs
- letter stickers
- pink ink pad
- scissors or other cutting tool
- ruler
- bone folder (optional)
- stapler with pink staples
- glue stick or other adhesive
- craft glue

Flowers, bling, and a sweet serenade—what more could a girl want on her special day? Your friend will hear you singing her praises with this sweet card.

Cut the black cardstock to 12" x 5¼" (30cm x 13.3cm), then score the center and fold to make a card that's 6" x 5¼" (15cm x 13.3cm).

Cut a piece of striped paper to 5¾" x 5" (14.6cm x 12.7cm). Cut out one portion of the birthday music paper, and tap the edges onto the pink ink pad. Staple the birthday paper, at an angle, onto the striped paper. Then center the striped paper on the card, adhering with the glue stick.

Use craft glue to adhere the flowers onto the card, placing three at the top left and two at the bottom right. Glue the gems onto their centers. Use the letter stickers to spell out the birthday girl's name. Add a gem to the name, if desired.

Happy 29th (again)

KRISTEN SWAIN

FLOWERED PAPER: Bob and Bob Studio • PEELING PAINT PAPER AND VELVET RIBBON: Flair Designs • GINGHAM RIBBON: Offray • LARGE LETTER STICKERS: American Crafts • SMALL LETTER STICKERS: Die Cuts With a View

WHAT YOU'LL NEED

- white cardstock
- black cardstock
- flowered paper
- pink peeling-paint patterned paper
- 3" (7.6cm) piece of pink gingham ribbon
- 3" (7.6cm) piece of pink velvet ribbon
- large orange letter stickers
- small pink letter stickers
- black fine-point pen
- scissors
- ruler
- paper trimmer (optional)
- bone folder (optional)
- glue stick

Have a girlfriend who is 30-something but refuses to age past 29? This brightly colored, tongue-in-cheek card will get her in a festive mood.

Cut the white cardstock to 8½" (22cm) square. Score the center of the card and fold to make a 4¼" x 8½" (11cm x 22cm) card.

Cut the flowered paper to 8" x 3¾" (20cm x 9.5cm). Glue onto black cardstock and trim the cardstock to leave a ⅛" (3mm) border. Position the white card with the fold on the top. Center the layered black cardstock onto the white card and glue in place.

Hand-draw a flower similar to those on the patterned paper onto the peeling-paint paper, using the black pen. Cut out the flower, cutting slightly outside the pen lines, and glue on the upper-left side of the card.

Cut a 1½" x 7½" (3.8cm x 19cm) strip from black cardstock and glue it over the bottom half of the pink flower, as shown. Place the letter stickers on the black strip and the flowered paper. Tie the two pieces of ribbon in a knot, and place in the flower center with a glue dot. Trim the ends.

BTW → by the way

IF YOU HAVE TROUBLE FINDING SMALL LETTER STICKERS, USE ALPHABET RUBBER STAMPS AND A BRIGHT INK COLOR. WHILE THE INK IS STILL WET, EMBOSS WITH CLEAR EMBOSSING POWDER FOR A SHINY FINISH.

Talk About Recycling

KELLY ANNE GRUNDHAUSER

CARDSTOCK: Paper Salon • PATTERNED PAPER: Mara-Mi • CUTTING SYSTEM: QuicKutz

WHAT YOU'LL NEED

- white cardstock
- wide-striped paper
- tone-on-tone striped paper
- aluminum sheet
- white acrylic paint
- pencil
- scissors
- ruler
- paper trimmer (optional)
- bone folder (optional)
- die-cutting system
- metal-distressing tool
- stylus
- paintbrush
- small flower punch
- glue stick or other adhesive
- craft glue
- paper towel

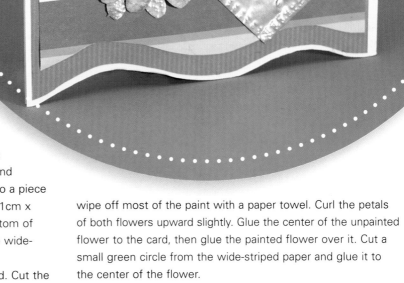

Cut the white cardstock to 9" x 5¼" (23cm x 13.3cm). Score and fold the center to create a card that's 4½" x 5¼" (11.5cm x 13.3cm).

Cut the wide-striped paper to 4" x 4½" (10cm x 11.5cm). With scissors, cut a wavy line at the top and bottom of the paper. With the glue stick, glue this to a piece of the tone-on-tone striped paper that is 4¼" x 5" (11cm x 12.7cm). Replicate the wavy line at the top and bottom of the tone-on-tone paper, creating a border above the wide-striped paper that is ¼" (6mm) wide.

Glue the layered piece to the center of the card. Cut the same wavy line on the cardstock, creating a ⅛" (3mm) border around the layered paper.

Use the die cutter to cut out *29 Again?* from the aluminum sheet. Glue the cutouts to the top of the card using craft glue.

Draw two 2" (5cm)-wide flowers on the aluminum. Cut out the flowers with scissors. Draw a 1⅝" x 2⅜" (4cm x 6cm) tag on the aluminum and cut it out with scissors.

Run the distressing tool over both the flowers. Lightly brush one of the flowers with white acrylic paint, then quickly wipe off most of the paint with a paper towel. Curl the petals of both flowers upward slightly. Glue the center of the unpainted flower to the card, then glue the painted flower over it. Cut a small green circle from the wide-striped paper and glue it to the center of the flower.

Run the distressing tool along the edges on the back side of the tag. Turn the tag to the front and lightly write *Talk about recycling!* on the tag with a pencil. Turn to the back of the tag again, and trace the lines of the words with the stylus. Use a good amount of pressure so that the words are legible from the front.

Use a small flower punch to punch a hole at the small end of the tag. Glue the tag to the card, slipping it under some of the flower petals.

shhh—It's a Surprise

LINDA BEESON

CARDSTOCK: Bazzill Basics • PATTERNED CARDSTOCK: Bo-Bunny Press • LARGE ALPHABET FOAM STAMPS: Making Memories • SMALL ALPHABET FOAM STAMPS: Li'l Davis • RUB-ON TRANSFERS: KI Memories • FLOWERS: Prima • PAINTS: Plaid

*This card features layers of fun—
all of which your friend will love
discovering to get to the gift inside.*

Cut a 10¾" x 5¼" (27cm x 13cm) strip from
the black/paisley cardstock. With a pencil,
make a mark 4" (10cm) from the left side
of the paper and 1¼" (3cm) from the right.
Score at each of these marks and fold the
ends toward the center with the black on the
outside.

Cut a 10½" x 5¼" (27cm x 13cm) strip from
the black/paisley cardstock. With a pencil, make a
mark 4" (10cm) from the left side of the paper and 1¼"
(3cm) from the right. Score at each of these marks and fold
the ends toward the center with the white on the outside.

Cut a 10" x 4" (25cm x 10cm) strip from the black cardstock. With a pencil, make a mark 4" (10cm) from one end
and 2" (5cm) from the other. Score at each mark and fold the
ends toward the center. With a sewing machine, sew the
smaller fold up to make a pocket for a gift card.

Ink the edges of the paisley, harlequin and white sides
of the folded strips with the black ink pad. Glue the harlequin
card inside the paisley card, so that the paisley card opens
to the sides and the harlequin card opens up and down. Glue
the folded black card inside the harlequin card.

Stamp *shhh* with white paint on the larger panel on the
front of the card. Stamp *surprise* with black paint on the large
white flap inside the card. Stamp *enjoy* with white paint on
the small flap of the inside pocket.

Cut a 3¼" (8cm) square from the harlequin cardstock and
a 2¾" (7cm) square from white cardstock; glue the two pieces
together. Use the rub-on letters to spell the inside sentiment
on the white cardstock. Attach two small flowers to the lower-
right corner of the white cardstock with a red brad. Glue this
layered piece to the front of the black flap.

Punch two ¾" (1.9cm) circles from paisley paper and two
1" (25mm) circles from black cardstock. Use the hole punch
to punch holes in the center of each. Also punch a hole on
each of the flaps on the front of the card, approximately ⅝"
(1.6cm) in from the edge of each flap. Insert an eyelet through
one paisley circle, one cardstock circle and through one side
of the card; then set the eyelet. Repeat with the other eyelet,
but this time catch one end of the ribbon under the eyelet
before setting. Use the ribbon to wrap around the other circle
to close the card.

Make a Wish

KELLY ANNE GRUNDHAUSER

WHAT YOU'LL NEED

- light blue cardstock
- brick red cardstock
- scraps of orange, yellow, green and blue cardstock
- striped paper
- flowered paper
- candles and text rubber stamp
- 6" (15cm) piece of large orange rickrack
- black ink pad
- Diamond Glaze
- sewing machine with black thread
- scissors
- ruler
- paper trimmer (optional)
- bone folder (optional)
- glue stick or other adhesive

Write wishes on the candles of this sunny card to help someone celebrate the season—her birthday season, that is. The rickrack hanger allows the card to be hung from a bulletin board for however long her season lasts.

LIGHT BLUE CARDSTOCK: Bazzill Basics • BRICK CARDSTOCK: Making Memories • CARDSTOCK SCRAPS AND PATTERNED PAPERS: Chatterbox • RUBBER STAMP: Paper Salon • RICKRACK: Queen & Company • DIAMOND GLAZE: JudiKins

Cut the light blue cardstock to 3¼" x 6⅝" (8.3cm x 16.8cm); cut a second piece to 2½" x 3" (6.4cm x 7.6cm). Cut the striped paper to 3" x 6½" (7.6cm x 16.5cm); cut the brick cardstock to 2⅛" x 3½" (5.4cm x 8.9cm); and cut the flowered paper to a 2⅞" (7.3cm) square.

Put glue on the bottom and sides of the small piece of blue cardstock. Glue it to the bottom of the brick red cardstock. Stack the brick red cardstock onto the striped paper and the striped paper onto the large piece of blue cardstock. Sew a zigzag stitch around the edge of the papers to secure them in place. Glue the flowered paper to the small blue cardstock.

Sew the rickrack to the top of the card with a zigzag stitch.

Cut a 1" x 4½" (2.5cm x 11.4cm) strip from each of the scrap pieces of cardstock. Stamp one candle at the end of each strip with black ink. Stamp the entire image on the flowered paper with black ink. When the ink is dry, apply Diamond Glaze to each candle and flame.

Happy Birthday
SHERRY WRIGHT

WHAT YOU'LL NEED

- pink cardstock
- brown cardstock
- blue cardstock
- paisley-patterned paper
- 7" (18cm) piece of blue velvet ribbon
- 3 blue paper flowers
- 3 blue gems
- birthday embellishment
- brown ink pad
- scissors or other cutting tool
- ruler
- bone folder (optional)
- 7/8" (2.2cm) circle cutter or paper punch
- BeJeweler tool
- glue stick or other adhesive

CARDSTOCK AND PATTERNED PAPER: Paper Salon • RIBBON: Fibers By The Yard • FLOWERS: Prima • GEMS: Swarovski • BIRTHDAY EMBELLISHMENT: Making Memories

A store-bought card can't be any prettier than this. It's perfect for a chic, sophisticated friend on her special day.

Cut the pink cardstock to 8½" x 5½" (22cm x 14cm), then score and fold to make a card that's 5½" x 4¼" (14cm x 11cm) with the fold at the top.

Cut a 5½" x 3" (14cm x 7.6cm) piece of paisley paper and glue it to the top of the card. Cut a 5½" x 1" (14cm x 2.5cm) strip of brown cardstock. Punch three evenly spaced circles in the brown cardstock and glue it to the bottom of the pink card.

Glue a paper flower inside each circle. Then adhere a gem to the center of each flower, using the BeJeweler tool.

Glue the ribbon where the paisley paper and brown cardstock meet, securing the ends on the inside of the card.

Cut a 2" x ½" (5cm x 1.3cm) piece of blue cardstock and ink the edges with the brown ink pad. Glue the birthday embellishment to the center, then glue the cardstock to the paisley paper, slightly left of center.

It's a Shower

NICOLE JACKSON

CARDSTOCK, PATTERNED PAPER AND RUBBER STAMPS: Paper Salon • RIBBON: SEI

WHAT YOU'LL NEED

- light blue cardstock
- white cardstock
- pink cardstock
- paisley-patterned paper
- camisole rubber stamp
- text rubber stamp
- 18" (46cm) piece of ⅝"-wide (1.6cm) brown ribbon
- brown ink pad
- pink watercolor pencil
- scissors or other cutting tool
- ruler
- bone folder (optional)
- ⅛" (3mm) hole punch
- glue stick or other adhesive

You've been bosom buddies since you started wearing training bras. Now it's time to celebrate her upcoming wedding with this sassy little number.

Cut the blue cardstock to 8½" x 5½" (22cm x 14cm), then score and fold to make a card that's 4¼" x 5½" (11cm x 14cm).

Stamp the camisole and text on white cardstock with brown ink. Color the hearts with watercolor pencil. Trim the camisole piece to 1¼" x 2" (3.2cm x 5cm) and the text piece to 2¼" x ½" (5.7cm x 1.3cm). Glue these pieces to pink cardstock, then trim the pink cardstock to leave a narrow border.

Cut two pieces of patterned paper: 5¼" x 2¾" (13cm x 7cm) and 5¼" x ¾" (13cm x 1.9cm). With the patterns running in the same direction, punch holes on the right side of the large piece and the left side of the small piece at ½", 1½", 2½", 3½", and 4½" (1.3cm, 3.8cm, 6.4cm, 8.9cm and 11.4cm) from the top (for a total of ten holes).

Lace the ribbon, starting at the top and back of the papers, all the way down to the bottoms, leaving a ½" (1.3cm) space between the two papers. Take care not to rip the papers. Tie a bow at the bottom and trim the ribbon ends.

Glue the patterned paper to the front of the blue card, still leaving the ½" (13mm) between the patterned papers. Glue the stamped pieces to the left of the ribbon.

Showers of Happiness
KELLY ANNE GRUNDHAUSER

WHAT YOU'LL NEED

- cardstock with four blocks of color
- pearl/circles double-sided patterned paper
- black fine-tip marker
- scissors
- ruler
- paper trimmer (optional)
- bone folder
- glue stick or other adhesive
- umbrella pattern, page 90

CARDSTOCK AND PATTERNED PAPER: Heidi Grace

Let that special bride- or mom-to-be know just how happy you are for her with this pretty card.

Cut and fold the cardstock to create a 5" (13cm) square card with 4" (10cm) of light pink showing on the top and 1" (3cm) of dark pink on the bottom.

Trace the umbrella pattern from page 90 onto the patterned side of the paper. Draw a 2½" (6cm) handle onto the pearl side of the paper. Cut out both pieces and glue on the front of the card.

With a bone folder, lightly score the sections of the umbrella to make creases from each scalloped point to the top of the umbrella. Using the black marker, dot an outline around the umbrella and handle and along each of the creases.

In your own hand, write the sentiment at the bottom of the card.

Wishing you Showers of Happiness!

BTW → by the way

JUST CAN'T BEAR TO HAND-WRITE ON YOUR CARDS? YOU CAN ALSO TYPE THE SENTIMENT ON YOUR COMPUTER OR SPELL IT OUT WITH RUB-ON TRANSFERS OR RUBBER STAMPS.

Bundle of Joy

ANABELLE O'MALLEY

WHAT YOU'LL NEED

- yellow cardstock
- green cardstock
- harlequin-patterned paper
- mesh
- baby carriage rubber stamp
- baby rattle rubber stamp
- pea pod baby rubber stamp
- text rubber stamp
- black ink pad
- green ink pad
- silver brad
- yellow and green colored pencils
- ruler
- bone folder (optional)
- 1" (2.5cm) circle punch
- corner rounder (optional)
- pinking shears or other decorative scissors
- scissors
- paper trimmer (optional)
- glue stick or other adhesive
- pop dots
- font: AL Anytime

Attach this hip card to a shower gift for the mom-to-be! It will make any recipient smile, and the bright colors can be used for boys or girls.

Cut the yellow cardstock to 8½" x 5½" (22cm x 14cm), then score and fold to make a card that's 5½" x 4¼" (14cm x 11cm) with the fold at the top.

Cut a piece of mesh to 5½" x 2" (14cm x 5cm) and glue it to the top of the card. Round the top corners of the card, including the mesh, with a corner rounder or scissors.

Cut a piece of harlequin paper to 5½" x 2½" (22cm x 6cm), and glue it to the bottom of the card. Print the sentiment on green cardstock, repeating it in one long line. Trim the card-stock to 5½" x ³⁄₈" (22cm x 9mm), cutting straight across the top and using pinking shears along the bottom. Glue this strip between the mesh and the harlequin paper, letting some words run off the edge of the card.

Glue a piece of mesh to yellow cardstock, then punch out three 1" (2.5cm) circles. Glue the circles to the patterned paper.

Stamp the carriage, rattle and pea pod images on white cardstock with black ink. Color the images with colored pencils, and trim around them. Glue the images over the circles.

Stamp the text onto white cardstock and trim to 2" x 1" (5cm x 2.5cm). Round the corners on one end of the cardstock, then ink all the edges with green ink. Insert a brad at one end and adhere the tag to the card with pop dots.

A Visit from the Stork

CHRISTINE DOYLE

WHAT YOU'LL NEED

- lime green cardstock
- orange cardstock
- red cardstock
- flowered paper
- tracing paper or vellum
- stork rubber stamp
- 4" (10cm) piece of red and white ribbon
- watermark stamp pad
- orange ink pad
- scissors or other cutting tool
- ruler
- bone folder (optional)
- paper trimmer (optional)
- glue stick
- double-sided tape

If your girlfriend is going to be a slightly untraditional kind of mom, then give her a slightly untraditional baby shower card. The tracing paper tones down the patterned paper a bit—but not too much.

GREEN AND ORANGE CARDSTOCK: Die Cuts With a View • FLOWERED PAPER: Me & My Big Ideas • RUBBER STAMP: A Muse Artstamps • RIBBON: Making Memories

Cut the green cardstock to 8" (20cm) square. Score and fold the center to create a card that's 4" x 8" (10cm x 20cm).

Cut the orange cardstock to 2⅝" x 3" (6.7cm x 7.6cm). Using the watermark stamp pad, stamp the image randomly over the cardstock, overlapping some images and running some off the edge of the paper. Wipe the stamp off, then ink it with the orange ink pad and stamp the image in the center of the orange cardstock. Glue the orange cardstock to the red cardstock and trim, leaving a ⅛" (3mm) border on all sides.

Cut the flowered paper to 4" x 5¾" (10cm x 14.6cm) and cut a piece of tracing paper or vellum to the same size. With bits of double-sided tape, adhere the tracing paper to the front of the flowered paper. Glue the flowered paper to the bottom part of the card.

Glue the ribbon to the top of the flowered paper. Glue the layered stamped image over the ribbon, aligning the baby's head with the ribbon.

BTW
by the way

WATERMARK STAMP PADS (LIKE THIS ONE FROM TSUKINEKO) CREATE AN IMAGE THAT'S JUST SLIGHTLY DARKER THAN THE COLOR OF YOUR PAPER. IT'S GREAT FOR CREATING A SUBTLE TONE-ON-TONE BACKGROUND THAT WILL MATCH YOUR DESIGN PERFECTLY.

Indulge

STACEY STAMITOLES

WHAT YOU'LL NEED

- premade black matchbook card with scalloped flap
- light pink cardstock
- pink dotted paper
- green dotted paper
- hot pink ribbon
- scissors or other cutting tool
- ruler
- bone folder (optional)
- 1/8" (3mm) hole punch
- slot punch
- glue stick or other adhesive
- font: Wendy Medium

Whether your friend is a new mom or has some other hectic job, she may not get pampered quite enough. Send her this card with a gift card inside so she won't have any excuse not to spend some time on herself.

Punch a hole in each scallop of the pre-made card with the hole punch. With the flap down, use the slot punch to punch holes 2" (5cm) in from the left edge of the flap and ¼" (6mm) down from the top of the flap. [The slot punch will punch two holes at once, placing them ¼" (6mm) apart]. Thread a 4" (10cm) piece of ribbon through the slots, securing the flap to the back of the card.

Cut the pink dotted paper to 4¼" (11cm) square and glue to the front of the card. Cut the green dotted paper to 3⅝" x 3⅛" (9.2cm x 7.9cm) and glue it to the pink dotted paper.

In your word processing program, create a text box. Type the greeting in the box, making the font color white and the background black. Print the text on the pink cardstock and trim leaving a thin border around the black box. Glue to the center of the green dots paper.

To include a gift certificate inside, cut a piece of ribbon to 5½" (14cm). Glue just the ends of the ribbon to the inside of the card and slip the gift certificate under the ribbon.

My Favorite Mom

LINDA BEESON

WHAT YOU'LL NEED

- coral cardstock
- green cardstock
- black cardstock
- 3 black-and-white patterned papers
- red heart brad
- text rub-on transfers
- black ink pad
- scissors
- ruler
- bone folder (optional)
- paper trimmer (optional)
- sewing machine with black thread
- 1" (2.5cm) circle punch or template
- 1¼" (3.2cm) circle punch or template
- 1¾" (4.5cm) circle punch or template
- glue stick or other adhesive

Is your mom one of your girlfriends? Let her know with this pretty card just for her.

Cut the coral cardstock to 8" x 9" (20cm x 23cm). Score and fold the center to make a card that's 4" x 9" (10cm x 23cm). Round all four corners with scissors or a corner rounder.

Stitch around the edge on the front of the card two times with the sewing machine. Ink the edges of the card with the ink pad.

Punch six 1¼" (3.2cm) circles from the patterned paper. Punch one 1¾" (4.5cm) circle from the black cardstock. Freehand cut a stem from the green cardstock and punch one 1¼" (3.2cm) circle and one 1" (2.5cm) circle for the leaves.

Sew the stem and the leaves to the front of the card, using zigzag and straight stitches. Form the flower by tucking the petal circles under the center circle. Sew around the center with a zigzag stitch, catching the edge of each petal to secure. Insert the heart brad in the lower right of the flower center.

Add the text rub-on tranfers to the bottom of the card.

BTW
by the way

TO KEEP THE FLOWER PIECES IN PLACE WHILE YOU'RE SEWING, GLUE THEM TO THE CARD FRONT WITH A LITTLE GLUE STICK. THEN THE STITCHING CAN BE PURELY DECORATIVE INSTEAD OF BEING THE ONLY THING HOLDING THE PIECES IN PLACE.

Spa Day

KELLY ANNE GRUNDHAUSER

CARDSTOCK, PATTERNED PAPERS AND RUBBER STAMP: Paper Salon • RIBBON: Offray • BRAD: Queen & Co. • FLOWER: Prima • RUB-ON TRANSFERS: C.R.Gibson • CHALKS: Pebbles

WHAT YOU'LL NEED

- pink cardstock
- brown cardstock
- white cardstock
- paisley-patterned paper
- button-patterned paper
- girl on a wall rubber stamp
- 8" (20cm) piece of pink and white ribbon, ⅛" (3mm) wide
- retailer gift-card tin
- large pink brad
- white flower
- brown ink pad
- alphabet rub-on transfers
- decorator chalks
- scissors or other cutting tool
- ruler
- bone folder (optional)
- sandpaper
- corner rounder (optional)
- glue stick or other adhesive
- craft glue

The tiny tin on the front of this card holds a gift card for a manicure, pedicure, facial, massage...or maybe all four! If you don't have a gift-card tin, use a small envelope.

Cut the pink cardstock to 8½" x 5½" (22cm x 14cm). Score the center and fold to create a card that's 5½" x 4¼" (14cm x 11cm) with the fold at the top. Cut a piece of paisley paper to 4½" x 3" (11.4cm x 7.6cm) and round the corners.

Cut the brown cardstock to 1¾" x 2⅛" (4.5cm x 5.4cm); round the corners. Stamp the girl on the white cardstock with brown ink. Trim the image to 1½" x 2" (3.8cm x 5cm), round the corners and color the image with chalks as desired. Glue the stamped image, centered on the brown cardstock.

Cut the ribbon to 5½" (14cm) and adhere it to the center of the card with craft glue. Center the paisley paper over the ribbon and glue in place. Glue the bottom of the tin to the center of the paisley paper with craft glue.

Glue a 2½" x 4" (6.4cm x 10cm) piece of button-patterned paper to the lid of the tin with glue stick. Sand off the excess paper and lightly rub the edges with chalk if you like. Center the brown cardstock on the button paper and glue in place.

Insert the brad through the center of the silk flower. Press out the flanges, then tie the remaining ribbon to the bottom of the brad. Using craft glue, attach the flower piece to the left side of the lid, creating a pull. Use the rub-on letters to write the sentiment of your choice on the pink card.

Girls' Night Out

STACEY STAMITOLES

- pink library pocket with insert
- off-white cardstock
- brown patterned paper with white dots
- text rub-on transfers
- flower rub-on transfers
- 7" (18cm) piece of flower trim ribbon
- scissors or other cutting tool
- ruler
- corner rounder (optional)
- glue stick or other adhesive
- glue lines

Know someone who just needs to get out? Gather up the girls with this snazzy invitation and have a wonderful evening of girl talk.

Trim the pink insert that comes with the pocket to 3³⁄₈" x 4¾" (8.6cm x 12.1cm). Round the top two edges of the insert with the corner rounder or with scissors.

Cut the brown patterned paper to 3¼" x 4½" (8.3cm x 11.4cm) and round the top two corners. Glue to the front of the insert. Trim the off-white cardstock to 2" x 3³⁄₈" (5cm x 8.6cm) and round the top two corners. Apply the text rub-on transfer and two of the flower rub-ons to the top of the off-white card. Then glue it to the front of the insert.

To decorate the front of the pocket, trim a piece of brown patterned paper to 3¼" x 2" (8.3cm x 5cm) and glue it to the center of the pocket. Trim a piece of pink cardstock

to 3³⁄₈" x 1¹⁄₈" (8.6cm x 2.9cm) and decorate it with rub-on dots and flowers. Glue this to the center of the brown dots paper, leaving a row of dots above and below the pink strip.

Cut two strips of flower trim to fit the width of the pocket and glue one above and one below the brown patterned paper with glue lines. Write the details for the invitation on the bottom of the off-white piece.

We ought to **celebrate** this hour by **expressions** of **joy.**

Ralph Waldo Emerson

You Go, Girl!

Giving congratulatory high-fives may not work for every friend in every situation, but one of the cards in this section definitely will. Whether your friend has just gotten a promotion or finally dumped her deadbeat boyfriend, nothing says "you go, girl" better than a handmade card.

Nice Move

LINDA BEESON

CARDSTOCK, PATTERNED PAPER AND RUBBER STAMP: Paper Salon • FONT: Two Peas in a Bucket

WHAT YOU'LL NEED

- green cardstock
- red cardstock
- ornament-patterned paper
- house rubber stamp
- flower brad
- green ink pad
- black ink pad
- scissors or other cutting tool
- ruler
- bone folder (optional)
- corner rounder (optional)
- 1¾" (4.5cm) circle punch
- glue stick
- font: Beautiful

Use this card to congratulate a friend on her new digs or a sweet social manuever. And, yes, this paper does come from a Christmas collection, but it's just too cool to use only once a year.

Cut the green cardstock to 8½" x 5½" (22cm x 14cm). Score and fold to create a card that's 5½" x 4¼" (14cm x 11cm) with the fold at the top.

Cut three 1½" x 3¾" (3.8cm x 9.5cm) strips from the ornament-patterned paper. Use a corner rounder or scissors to round all the corners. Ink the edges of the strips with the green ink pad.

Glue the ornament strips to red cardstock, and trim the cardstock to leave a narrow border on each side of the strips. Round the corners to match the ornament paper.

Stamp the house onto green cardstock with black ink. Punch out the house with the circle punch. Glue the circle to red cardstock and trim to leave a thin border. Insert the flower brad over the flower on the stamped image.

Print the text on green cardstock and cut it out, rounding the edges. Glue this piece to red cardstock, and trim to leave a thin border.

Glue the ornament paper strips onto the card, then the text and the image.

BTW → by the way

NO ONE HAS TO KNOW THE SECRETS TO MAKING A HANDMADE CARD. HIDE RIBBON ENDS, BRAD FLANGES OR THREAD FROM SEWING BY GLUING A PANEL THAT MATCHES THE CARDSTOCK ONTO THE INSIDE LEFT OF THE CARD.

Way to Go

MIKI BENEDICT

CARDSTOCK AND PATTERNED PAPERS: Paper Salon • RIBBON: Offray • STICKERS: KI Memories

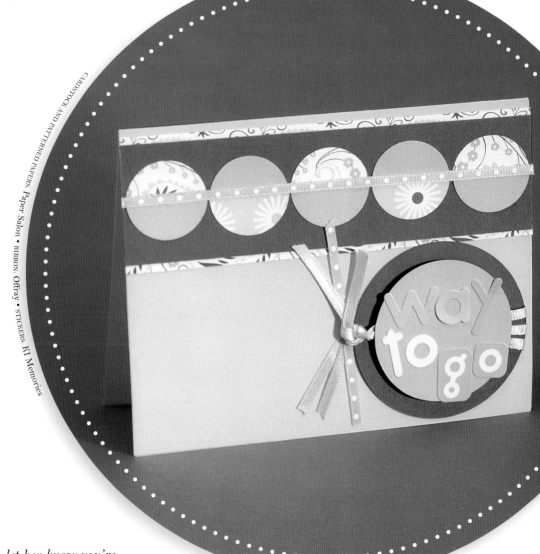

WHAT YOU'LL NEED

- pink cardstock
- brown cardstock
- light blue cardstock
- green cardstock
- paisley-patterned paper
- flowered paper
- 14½" (37cm) piece of pink ribbon with white dots
- 9" (23cm) piece of green ribbon
- 9" (23cm) piece of blue ribbon
- alphabet stickers
- scissors or other cutting tool
- ruler
- bone folder (optional)
- 1" (2.5cm) circle punch
- 2" (5cm) circle template
- 2½" (6.4cm) circle template
- glue stick
- glue dots
- foam mounting tape

Give your girlfriend a card to let her know you're behind her 100 percent. When making this card, check the bottom of your paper punch to see if there are alignment marks that can make punching semicircles from the edge of the paper a snap.

Cut the pink cardstock to 8½" x 5½" (22cm x 14cm). Score and fold to create a card that's 5½" x 4¼" (14cm x 11cm), with the fold at the top.

Cut a 1½" x 5½" (3.8cm x 14cm) piece of brown cardstock and glue it to a 1¾" x 5½" (4.5cm x 14cm) piece of paisley paper. Glue to the top front of the pink cardstock.

Punch 1" (2.5cm) circles from the blue cardstock, green cardstock, paisley paper and flowered paper. Cut the patterned circles in half, then glue the flowered semicircles to the green circles and the paisley semicircles to the blue circles. Glue the circles to the brown strip as shown. Cut the pink ribbon to 5½" (14cm) and glue over the centers of the circles.

Use templates to cut a 2½" (6.4cm) circle from brown cardstock and a 2" (5cm) circle from green cardstock. Wrap the remaining pink ribbon and the blue and green ribbon around the brown circle, tying a knot at one edge. Use glue dots as needed to secure the ribbons. Glue the brown circle to the lower-right corner of the card. Use stickers to spell the sentiment on the green circle, then adhere the green circle to the brown circle with foam tape.

A Toast for You

JENNIFER ELLEFSON

WHAT YOU'LL NEED

- white cardstock
- light blue cardstock
- assorted patterned papers
- white printer paper
- toasting-woman rubber stamp
- 9" (23cm) piece of light blue rickrack
- brown ink pad
- colored pencils
- scissors or other cutting tool
- ruler
- bone folder (optional)
- glue stick
- repositionable tape
- foam mounting tape

Cut the white cardstock to 8½" x 5½" (22cm x 14cm). Score and fold to create a card that's 5½" x 4¼" (14cm x 11cm) with the fold at the top.

Cut four different patterned papers to 2" x 2½" (5cm x 6.4cm). Arrange the pieces onto the front of the card, overlapping the edges in the center; glue the papers in place. Cut two pieces of rickrack: one to fit the width of patterned papers and another to fit the length. Glue these over the overlapping edges of patterned paper.

Stamp the toasting image on white cardstock with brown ink. Trim the cardstock to 1⅛" x 2¼" (2.9cm x 5.7cm), then ink the edges with the brown ink pad. Color in the image with colored pencils.

Cut the blue cardstock to 1⅜" x 3" (3.5cm x 7.6cm). Use your computer to print the text on white printer paper. Then adhere the blue cardstock to the paper with repositionable tape, aligning the cardstock so the text will print where desired. Print the sentiment again on the same piece of paper (this time it will print on the blue cardstock), and remove the cardstock from the paper.

Glue the stamped image on the blue cardstock and adhere it to the center of the card with foam tape.

BTW › *by the way* ‹

A RUBBER STAMP IS A TERRIFIC JUMPING OFF POINT FOR YOUR CARDS. AS THESE TWO CARDS SHOW, YOU CAN ADD PAPERS AND EMBELLISHMENTS TO GIVE ANY STAMP A VERY DIFFERENT LOOK.

Cheers!

NICOLE JACKSON

WHAT YOU'LL NEED

- yellow cardstock
- white cardstock
- teal cardstock
- harlequin-patterned paper
- flowered paper
- toasting-woman rubber stamp
- text rubber stamp
- 7" (18cm) piece of green ribbon
- 3 adhesive gems
- black ink pad
- watercolor pencils
- scissors or other cutting tool
- ruler
- bone folder (optional)
- hole punch
- glue stick or other adhesive
- glue dots

CARDSTOCK, PATTERNED PAPER AND RUBBER STAMPS: Paper Salon • GEMS: Carolee's Creations

Know someone who deserves a champagne toast? Whether it's for a fabulous new job or just a brand-new do, this card will help her celebrate.

Cut the yellow cardstock to 8½" x 5½" (22cm x 14cm). Score and fold to create a card that's 4¼" x 5½" x (11cm x 14cm).

Cut the harlequin paper to 3" x 4¼" (7.6cm x 10.8cm) and the flower paper to 3¼" x 4¼" (8.3cm x 10.8cm). Glue the flower paper to the lower right of the card about ⅛" (3mm) from the side and bottom edges. Glue the harlequin paper to the upper left of the card, about ⅛" (3mm) from the top and side edges. The harlequin paper will overlap the flower paper.

Stamp the image and text onto white cardstock with black ink, and color the image with watercolor pencils. Trim the image to 1" x 2¼" (2.5cm x 5.7cm) and the text to 2¼" x ¾" (5.7cm x 1.9cm). Glue the image to a piece of teal cardstock and trim, leaving a narrow border. Glue to the front of the card.

Punch a hole on both ends of the sentiment, about ¼" (6mm) from the edge. Tie a 3" (8cm) piece of ribbon through the left hole, and a 4" (10cm) piece of ribbon through the right. Glue the sentiment about ¾" (1.9cm) from the bottom and left edges of the card. Adhere the ribbon ends to the back and inside of the card using glue dots.

Adhere the jewels in the upper left, placing the first in the center of a diamond, the second at an intersection of two diamonds, and the third again in the center.

Congratulations

STACEY STAMITOLES

WHAT YOU'LL NEED

- bright pink cardstock
- brown cardstock
- white cardstock
- striped paper
- flowered paper
- text rubber stamp
- 3 small paper flowers
- bright pink ink pad
- scissors or other cutting tool
- ruler
- bone folder (optional)
- sewing machine with brown thread
- glue stick or other adhesive
- craft glue
- pearly dimensional adhesive

Hip, hip, hooray! Send this fun and funky card to a girlfriend for any celebration occasion.

Cut the pink cardstock to 8½" x 5½" (22cm x 14cm). Score and fold to create a card that's 5½" x 4¼" (14cm x 11cm) with the fold at the top.

Cut the brown cardstock to 5½" x 4⅛" (14cm x 10.5cm) and glue it, centered, onto the front of the card. Trim the striped paper to 5½" x 3¾" (14cm x 9.5cm) and center it on the brown cardstock. Cut the flowered paper to 5½" x 3" (14cm x 7.6cm) and center it on the striped paper.

Stamp the sentiment on white cardstock using the pink ink pad. Trim the white cardstock to 3½" x 1¼" (8.9cm x 3.2cm). Glue the white cardstock to pink cardstock, and trim to leave a ⅛" (3mm) border. Glue the pink cardstock onto brown, and again trim to leave a ⅛" (3mm) border. Sew around the edges of the white cardstock using the zigzag stitch on your sewing machine. Glue the layered sentiment on the front of the card.

Use craft glue to attach the three paper flowers in the upper-right corner of the layered text. Add a drop of pearly adhesive to the center of each and let dry.

BTW
by the way

DON'T BE AFRAID TO MIX AND MATCH UNUSUAL PATTERNS AND COLORS WHEN YOU MAKE CARDS. LET THE MIX BE A REFLECTION OF YOU!

Enjoy!

LINDA BEESON

- blue cardstock
- black cardstock
- white cardstock
- slide mount
- 4 assorted coordinating patterned papers
- text rub-on tranfers
- blue silk flower
- brown brad
- black ink pad
- scissors or other cutting tool
- ruler
- bone folder (optional)
- sewing machine with black thread (optional)
- glue stick or other adhesive
- craft glue

When your girlfriend has achieved the riches she deserves, remind her to take the time to ... enjoy!

Cut a piece of blue cardstock to 5¼" x 10½" (13.5cm x 27cm). Score and fold to create a card that's 5¼" (13.5cm) square.

Cut the white cardstock to a 4½" (11.4cm) square, then ink the edges on the black ink pad. Cut the black cardstock to a 4¾" (12.1cm) square, and glue the white cardstock to the black. Glue this layered piece to the front of the card.

Cut the patterned papers into pieces 1¼" (4.5cm) wide and anywhere from ¾" to 1" (1.9cm to 2.5cm) tall. Ink the edges of the papers, then glue them in two columns on the left side of the card. Accent the centers of the columns with black thread in a zigzag stitch, if you like.

Cover the slide mount with one of the patterned papers and ink the edges with the black ink pad. Cut a piece of white cardstock to fit inside the slide mount. Apply a rub-on transfer to the cardstock, then sandwich the paper between the front and back of the mount. Insert the brad in the center of the flower. With craft glue, attach the flower to the bottom-right corner of the slide mount and glue the slide mount to the card. Apply a second rub-on transfer to the bottom-right corner of the card.

Bon Voyage

LINDA BEESON

CARDSTOCK, PATTERNED PAPER AND RUBBER STAMP: Paper Salon • BRADS: Making Memories • FONT: Two Peas in a Bucket

WHAT YOU'LL NEED

- green cardstock
- white cardstock
- brown cardstock
- harlequin-patterned paper
- Eiffel Tower rubber stamp
- 3 brads
- black ink pad
- brown ink pad
- scissors or other cutting tool
- ruler
- paper trimmer (optional)
- bone folder (optional)
- glue stick or other adhesive
- foam mounting tape
- font: Falling Leaves

Congratulate a friend on booking the vacation of her dreams with this sunny card. Let her know you're proud of her ... and maybe a little jealous.

Cut the green cardstock to 8½" x 5½" (22cm x 14cm). Score and fold to create a card that's 5½" x 4¼" (14cm x 11cm) with the fold at the top.

Stamp the Eiffel Tower image on white cardstock with black ink. Trim the image to 1¾" x 2½" (4.5cm x 6.4cm), then ink the edges with the brown ink pad.

Glue the image to green cardstock and trim to leave a narrow border. Ink the edges with the brown ink pad. Glue the layered piece onto the brown cardstock and again trim to leave a narrow border.

Cut the harlequin paper to 4¾" x 3" (12.1cm x 7.6cm) and ink the edges with brown ink. Glue this onto a piece of brown cardstock and trim to leave a ⅛" (3mm) border.

Print the text on white cardstock. Cut the phrases to size and ink around the edges with brown ink.

Layer the *you go girl* piece onto green cardstock and then onto brown cardstock, each time trimming to leave a narrow border.

Glue the text pieces to the right side of the card, then insert brads into one end of each small piece. Attach the stamped image on the left side of the card using foam tape.

Clap, Clap, Clap

LINDA BEESON

WHAT YOU'LL NEED

- striped/flowered double-sided cardstock
- white cardstock
- light blue cardstock
- brown cardstock
- light brown cardstock
- envelope template
- black ink pad
- scissors or other cutting tool
- ruler
- bone folder (optional)
- glue stick or other adhesive
- fonts: Vintage Typewriter, University, Miss, Stencil

For those occasions when a round of applause is most suitable, send this card that says it with style.

Cut the double-sided cardstock to 6½" x 7½" (16.5cm x 19cm). With the paper horizontal on your work surface, flowered side up, score lines at 2½" (6.4cm) from the left edge and 2¼" (5.7cm) from the right. Fold both ends inward to make a trifold card with the flowers on the inside.

On your computer, create one text box that reads *applause* and *clap* and a second that reads *you did it!* Repeat the text in each box, using different fonts. (Type the words in individual text boxes to make the words overlap.) Print both boxes on white cardstock. Trim each box and glue to blue cardstock. Trim the blue cardstock, leaving a narrow border. Then glue the blue cardstock onto brown cardstock and trim again, leaving a narrow border. Glue the layered squares to the front and inside center panels of the card.

To make the envelope, repeat *clap* in different fonts on your computer, then print this onto the light brown cardstock. Trace the envelope template on the cardstock. Cut out the envelope and fold where indicated. Glue the envelope together, then ink the edges of the envelope with the black ink pad.

BTW by the way

INSTEAD OF CREATING THE TEXT FOR THE CARD AND ENVELOPE ON THE COMPUTER, STAMP THE TEXT USING DIFFERENT ALPHABET STAMP SETS AND THE BLACK INK PAD.

Charm

ANNA ARMENDARIZ

WHAT YOU'LL NEED

- pink cardstock
- harlequin-patterned paper
- wavy-striped paper
- white paper
- green paper
- lavender paper
- small pink gem
- swirls rubber stamp
- pink ink pad
- black pen
- scissors
- ruler
- paper trimmer (optional)
- bone folder (optional)
- glue stick or other adhesive

Everyone loves to be reminded how charming they are—especially someone who has worked her charm to her advantage.

CARDSTOCK, PATTERNED PAPERS AND RUBBER STAMP: Paper Salon • GEM: Heidi Swapp • WRITING PEN: EK Success

a way of getting the answer yes — without having asked any particular question.
~ Albert Camus

Cut the pink cardstock to 8½" x 5½" (22cm x 14cm). Score and fold to create a card that's 4¼" x 5½" (11cm x 14cm).

Cut a 3" x 5½" (7.6cm x 14cm) piece of harlequin paper. Cut along one of the wavy lines in the striped paper for a strip that's ¾" x 5½" (1.9cm x 14cm). Glue the wavy stripe behind the right long edge of the harlequin paper so that ½" (1.3cm) of the wavy design shows from the front. Glue the patterned paper to the front of the card, placing the left edge ⅛" (3mm) from the card fold.

Stamp the white paper with the swirl image and pink ink. Freehand draw a flower and cut it out. Cut a stem from green paper and a ¾" (1.9cm) circle from lavender paper. Glue the flower pieces to the front of the card.

Use the black pen to roughly outline the petals and center of the flower. Then write the text on the outside and inside of the card (see inside text at right). Finish by gluing the gem to the center of the flower.

Celebrate

TONIA DAVENPORT

WHAT YOU'LL NEED

- yellow cardstock
- yellow paper
- kaleidoscope-patterned paper
- yellow-and-gold striped paper
- text rub-on transfer
- 7" (18cm) piece of white rickrack
- red ink pad
- scissors
- paper trimmer (optional)
- bone folder or craft stick
- craft knife
- cutting mat
- glue stick or other adhesive
- craft glue

Whether your friend landed a new job, received an overdue award, or finally has her house back now that her son is going off to college, encourage her to celebrate!

Trim a piece of yellow cardstock to 8½" x 5½" (22cm x 14cm), then score and fold to make a card that's 4¼" x 5½" (11cm x 14cm). Trim the kaleidoscope paper to 4" x 5¼" (10cm x 14cm) and glue it to the front of the card.

Apply the rub-on transfer to the yellow paper and trim, leaving a thin yellow edge around the text. Using a glue stick, adhere the text to the striped paper so that it runs parallel with the stripes. Trim the striped paper to ⅝" x 2¾" (1.6cm x 7cm), and then round the corners using scissors.

Use the craft knife to cut two pairs of ⅜" (1cm) slits, one pair on either side of the text, through the striped paper. Ink the edges of the striped paper with the red ink pad. Let dry.

Cut one piece of white rickrack to 2½" (6.4cm). Thread it through the slits in the striped paper so just a bit of rickrack appears on each side of the text. Glue the ends to the back of the text with craft glue and trim the excess.

Cut four 1" (2.5cm) pieces of rickrack. Align two pieces on each side of the sentiment, positioning them just above and below the threaded rickrack. Glue the ends to the back of the sentiment. Glue the sentiment to the center of the card.

Trim the ends of the rickrack flush with the edges of the card, then dab craft glue onto the ends to secure them to the card and to keep the ends from fraying.

Groovy Chick

JEANETTE BESHEARS

WHAT YOU'LL NEED

- red cardstock
- turquoise cardstock
- gold cardstock
- yellow cardstock
- black cardstock
- harlequin-patterned paper
- light-denim-patterned paper
- small-flowered paper
- denim-patchwork-patterned paper
- small round puffy stickers
- mini brads
- 4 acrylic gems

- foam flip-flops
- ruler
- detail scissors
- paper trimmer
- bone folder (optional)
- daisy paper punches in three sizes
- mini flower paper punch
- 1/8" (3mm) hole punch

- glue stick or other adhesive
- craft glue
- patterns on page 90

With its mod daisies, bell–bottom blue jeans and long vest, this card screams '60s, a time when everyone was feeling groovy. Send it to offer congratulations to a girlfriend for getting her groove back.

Cut the red cardstock to 9½" x 6¾" (24cm x 27cm). Score and fold the center to create a card that's 4¾" x 6¾" (12cm x 17cm).

Cut the turquoise cardstock to 4⅝" x 6⅝" (11.8cm x 16.8cm) and the gold cardstock to 4½" x 6½" (11.4cm x 16.5cm). Cut a piece of harlequin paper to 4¼" x 6¼" (10.8cm x 15.9cm). Glue the gold cardstock onto the red with glue stick. Tear the harlequin paper diagonally into three pieces and glue the corners to the yellow cardstock.

Create layered daisies using the flower punches and red, turquoise and yellow cardstock. Punch black cardstock daisies the same size as the bottom layer of each flower. Glue one to the bottom of each layered daisy, slightly off center, to give a shadow effect. Place a puffy sticker in the center of each large daisy and a brad in the center of each small daisy. Glue the daisies to the harlequin paper, leaving space for the clothes in the center of the card.

Copy the clothes patterns from page 90. Cut out the patterns and trace them onto the paper with the front of the pattern face down on the back side of the paper. Cut the pants out of light denim paper. Cut the blouse out of flowered paper and the blouse trim from red cardstock. Cut the vest from turquoise cardstock and the purse pieces from denim-patchwork paper.

Glue the purse pieces onto red cardstock and trim, leaving a narrow border. Assemble the outfit and the purse on black cardstock and glue in place. Trim each leaving a narrow black border. Punch four mini flowers and embellish the center of each with a gem, adhering them with craft glue. Embellish the vest, pants and purse with these mini flowers.

Glue the outfit and purse to the harlequin paper, overlapping some of the daisies. Glue on the flip-flops and add another punched daisy over the purse if you like. Trim any daisy petals that extend beyond the rectangular turquoise border. Glue the layered piece to the front of the card.

For the inside of the card, layer the turquoise, gold and harlequin papers as you did above, but do not tear the harlequin paper. Glue these to the inside of the card.

Print your sentiment onto gold cardstock. Trim the cardstock to 3¼" x 4½" (8.3cm x 11.4cm) and round the corners. Layer this onto a 4¾" x 5" (12.1cm x 12.7cm) piece of turquoise cardstock. Round the corners on the turquoise cardstock and glue it to the center of the harlequin paper. Create a large flower from red, turquoise and gold cardstock. Glue the flower to the upper left of the sentiment and place a puffy sticker in the center of the flower.

Expressions of Joy

LINDA BEESON

WHAT YOU'LL NEED

- purple/striped double-sided cardstock
- cardstock with quote
- 4" (10cm) piece of orange ribbon
- purple chalk pad
- scissors
- ruler
- paper trimmer (optional)
- bone folder (optional)
- corner rounder (optional)
- sewing machine with green thread
- 1/8" (3mm) hole punch
- glue stick or other adhesive
- foam mounting tape

Send this card to a friend to encourage her to celebrate her special accomplishment, expressing joy however she sees fit.

Cut a 6" x 12" (15cm x 30cm) piece of double-sided cardstock. Score and fold to create a card that's 6" (15cm) square, with the purple on the outside. Ink the edges of the front of the card with the purple chalk pad.

Cut a 5½" (14cm) square from the same paper and round the corners with a corner rounder or scissors. Ink the edges of the square. Glue the square to the card with the stripes showing, then sew around the square to accent.

Draw a flower on another piece of cardstock with a pencil [my flower is approximately 5½" (14cm) across]. Cut

out the flower and ink the purple side of it with the chalk pad. Glue the flower off-center to the front of the card, then sew around the petals with the sewing machine.

Ink the edges of the quote cardstock with the chalk pad, and punch a hole in the lower left side. Thread one end of the ribbon through the hole and tie a knot. Adhere the quote piece to the center of the flower with foam tape.

Funky Flowers

SHERRY WRIGHT

CARDSTOCK AND PATTERNED PAPER: Paper Salon • RICKRACK: Fibers By The Yard • SILK FLOWER: Prima • GEM: Swarovski • TWILL EMBELLISHMENT: Making Memories • SMALL FLOWER DIE CUTTER: QuicKutz

WHAT YOU'LL NEED

- green cardstock
- lilac cardstock
- periwinkle cardstock
- circle-patterned paper
- 7" (18cm) piece of light blue rickrack
- small silk flower
- gems
- twill sentiment embellishment
- periwinkle ink pad
- green ink pad
- scissors
- ruler
- paper trimmer (optional)
- bone folder (optional)
- sewing machine with lilac thread (optional)
- flower die-cut system or templates (optional)
- BeJeweler tool
- glue stick or other adhesive
- craft glue

Even in today's computer world, a simple e-mail congrats simply won't do. Tell your girlfriend how proud you are of her special accomplishment with flowers—funky flowers, that is!

Cut the green cardstock to 8½" x 5½" (22cm x 14cm). Score and fold to create a card that's 5½" x 4¼" (14cm x 11cm). Cut a strip of lilac cardstock to 4¼" x ½" (10.8cm x 1.3cm) and glue it to the card so that the top edge of the strip is about 1½" (3.8cm) from the bottom of the card.

Glue the rickrack below the lilac strip, wrapping the right end around the inside of the card. Sew around the front of the card, if desired.

Freehand cut flowers of various sizes or use a die-cut system. I cut my flowers as follows: one at 3⅞" (9.8cm) from the circle paper, one at 2¾" (7cm) and one at 1" (2.5cm) from the periwinkle cardstock, one at 1⅞" (4.8cm) from the lilac cardstock, and one at 1" (2.5cm) from the green cardstock. Ink the edges of the flowers with the periwinkle and green ink pads, and glue the flowers onto the card.

With craft glue, attach the silk flower to the center of the front-most flower, then use the BeJeweler tool to adhere the gem to the flower center. Glue the twill embellishment on the right side of the lilac strip.

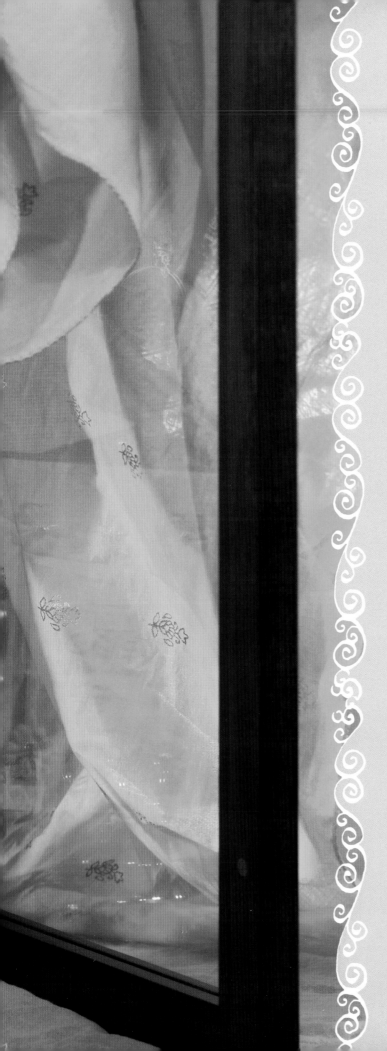

Best Friends Forever

Remember passing notes
in junior high signed *BFF*?
Whether you still sign your
notes like this or not, you
probably have a better idea now
of what a Best Friend Forever
really is. In this section you're
sure to find the perfect card to
express why your girlfriends
today truly are your BFFs.

A True Friend Tells You...

KELLY ANNE GRUNDHAUSER

A true friend tells you about the toilet paper on your shoe.

WHAT YOU'LL NEED

- lavender cardstock
- brown cardstock
- circle-patterned paper
- flowered paper
- Diamond Glaze
- toilet paper
- brown ink pad
- scissors
- ruler
- bone folder (optional)
- glue stick or other adhesive
- craft glue
- pattern on page 91

Everyone knows that feeling of looking in the mirror and seeing something in your teeth or on your face. This card addresses another one of those embarrassing situations when it's good to have a friend around.

Cut the lavender cardstock to 8½" x 5½" (22cm x 14cm). Score and fold the center to create a card that's 5½" x 4¼" (14cm x 11cm) with the fold at the top.

Print the text on lavender cardstock and trim to approximately 2" x ⅞" (5cm x 2.2cm). Layer this onto a piece of circle-patterned paper cut to 3" x 2" (7.6cm x 5cm). Then layer this piece on a piece of flowered paper cut to 3¼" x 4" (8cm x 10cm). Glue this to the left side of the card.

Trace the shoe pattern from page 91 onto brown cardstock. Cut out the shoe and apply Diamond Glaze to the heel and sole. Let dry, then glue the shoe to the right side of the card. Ink the edges of the card with the brown ink pad.

Cut a ½" (1cm) wide piece of toilet paper and tie it into a knot. Glue it to the top of the circle-patterned paper with craft glue. Accordion fold a square of toilet paper to a triangle shape as shown. Spread a light layer of craft glue on the heel of the shoe and along the bottom of the card; adhere the toilet paper to the glue.

Luv Ya, Girl

CINDY CURTIS

CARDSTOCK: DMD Industries • PATTERNED PAPERS: Sassafras Lass • WINDOW MOUNT: Deluxe Designs • VELVET AND STRIPED RIBBON: Flair Designs • SHEER RIBBON: May Arts • ALPHABET STICKERS: Doodlebug Design • METAL HEART: Making Memories

WHAT YOU'LL NEED

- light brown cardstock
- 4 coordinated patterned papers
- 4¼" (10.8cm) square window mount
- 5" (13cm) piece of pink-and-brown striped ribbon
- 5" (13cm) piece of pink velvet ribbon
- metal heart embellishment
- alphabet stickers
- scissors
- ruler
- bone folder (optional)
- corner rounder (optional)
- glue stick or other adhesive

Want to do something sweet for your best friend? Buy her a gift certificate and tuck it inside this fun card. She is sure to "luv" them both!

Cut the light brown cardstock to 12" x 6" (30cm x 15cm). Score and fold the cardstock to create a 6" (15cm) square card with the fold at the top. Round all four corners with scissors or a corner rounder.

Cut squares of patterned paper to 1¾" (4.5cm). Tie the velvet and striped ribbons to the outer edges of the window mount, as shown. Run a glue stick on the back of the window mount, and adhere the papers so they face out through the front of the window. Use craft glue to adhere the window to the front of the card.

Tie the sheer ribbon to the heart embellishment, then glue it in the upper-left square. Use letter stickers to spell your text.

BTW
by the way

THE FOUR QUADRANTS OF THE WINDOW OFFER POSSIBILITIES FOR MANY COLOR SCHEMES FOR ANY OCCASION. PICK PAPERS THAT USE A FRIEND'S FAVORITE COLORS OR ONES THAT FIT A THEME.

Friends are Flowers

KELLY ANNE GRUNDHAUSER

WHAT YOU'LL NEED

- yellow cardstock
- flowered paper
- striped paper
- self-adhesive cotton fabric
- 2 paper flowers
- 2 large gems
- scissors or other cutting tool
- ruler
- bone folder (optional)
- sewing machine with orange thread
- glue stick or other adhesive
- craft glue

Send this sunny card to the flowers in your life, thanking them for helping you through a rough patch— or for no reason at all.

Cut the yellow cardstock to 8½" x 5½" (22cm x 14cm). Score and fold the center to create a card that's 4¼" x 5½" (11cm x 14cm).

Cut the flowered paper to 4¼" x 2" (11cm x 5cm) and glue it to the top of the card. Cut the striped paper to 4¼" x 3" (11cm x 7.6cm) and glue to the bottom of the card.

Print the text onto the self-adhesive fabric. Trim and adhere to a piece of yellow cardstock. Cut the cardstock, leaving a ¼" (6mm) border around the sentiment. Sew a flower border across the top and bottom of the cardstock. Glue this between the patterned papers on the front of the card.

Glue a paper flower to each side of the text and adhere a gem to each flower center with craft glue.

Road to a Friend's House

LINDA BEESON

CARDSTOCK: Bazzill Basics and Prism • PATTERNED PAPER: Basic Grey • FOAM STAMP: Plaid • RUBBER STAMP: A Muse Artstamps • PEARL EX: Jacquard

WHAT YOU'LL NEED

- red cardstock
- turquoise cardstock
- white cardstock
- plaid paper
- large foam stamp
- text rubber stamp
- black ink pad
- Pearl Ex powder
- Pearl Ex varnish
- scissors or other cutting tool
- ruler
- bone folder (optional)
- disposable plate
- foam brush
- glue stick or other adhesive
- foam tape

Cut the red cardstock to 5¼"x 10½" (13.5cm x 27cm). Score and fold the center to make a 5¼" (13.5cm) square card with the fold at the top.

Cut a 4¾" (12.1cm) square from the turquoise cardstock and a 4⅝" (11.8cm) square from the plaid paper. Glue the plaid square over the turquoise square and glue to the card front.

Mix a small amount of Pearl Ex powder and varnish on a disposable plate. Brush the mixture onto the foam stamp with the foam brush. Stamp the image on white cardstock. When dry, tear around the image and glue on top of the plaid paper.

Stamp the text in black ink on white cardstock. Trim around the sentiment and glue to a piece of turquoise cardstock. Trim the turquoise cardstock, leaving a narrow border. Adhere the text to the front of the card with foam tape.

I'd Pick You

KELLY ANNE GRUNDHAUSER

WHAT YOU'LL NEED

- white cardstock
- teal cardstock
- large-flowered paper
- small flower rubber stamp
- clear cellophane
- light blue ink pad
- Diamond Glaze
- scissors
- ruler
- bone folder (optional)
- corner rounder (optional)
- sewing machine with green thread
- glue stick or other adhesive

Sending a bouquet of flowers has never been easier or less expensive— and watering is not required.

Cut the white cardstock to 8½" x 5½" (22cm x 14cm). Score and fold the center to create a card that's 4¼" x 5½" (11cm x 14cm). Trim ⅞" (2.2cm) from the right side of the front panel of the card. Use the corner rounder or scissors to round the four corners on the right side of the card.

Lightly stamp the flower image with blue ink randomly over the front of the card and around the edges of the inside panel. Ink the edges of the card with the blue ink pad.

In the center of the front panel, sew five different stems, ranging in height from 2" to 3¾" (5cm to 9.5cm). Cut out the shape of a vase from clear cellophane. Place the vase over the stems, then use the Diamond Glaze to secure the vase on the sides, top and bottom.

Cut five different flowers from the patterned paper. Place glue in the center only of each flower and glue to the top of the stems. Curl the petals up slightly.

Print the text out on teal cardstock and cut out each word. Glue these down the right inside panel of the card.

BTW
by the way

INSTEAD OF PURCHASING CLEAR CELLOPHANE FOR THE VASE, JUST USE CLEAR PACKAGING THAT YOU WOULD HAVE THROWN AWAY ANYWAY. EITHER WILL GIVE THE LOOK OF A CLEAR VASE FULL OF WATER.

Precious

LINDA BEESON

Sometimes a single word is all you need to describe a cherished friendship in a heartfelt way.

Cut the brown/striped cardstock to 5¾" x 11½" (15cm x 30cm). Score and fold the center to create a card that's 5¾" (15cm) square, with the fold at the top.

Cut a 5½" (14cm) square from the turquoise double-sided cardstock. Cut a 5" (13cm) square from the brown/striped cardstock. Ink the edges of the striped side of the cardstock with the brown chalk pad. Glue this square to the turquoise square. Glue this to the front of the card.

Use a template to cut a heart from the brown side of the cardstock, or freehand draw a heart and cut it with scissors. Sand the edges of the heart and the edges of the folded card with sandpaper. Glue the heart to the front of the card.

Cut the text panel from the cardstock. Glue this onto the turquoise side of the cardstock and trim to leave a narrow border. Glue this onto the brown side of the cardstock and trim again, leaving a narrow border. Glue this over the heart.

Punch a hole on one side of the text layered panel with the anywhere punch. Punch a second hole about ³⁄₈" (1cm) from the first on the striped part of the card. Repeat on the other side of the text panel.

Cut the ribbon in half and thread one end of each piece of ribbon up through the holes on one side of the panel and tie a knot. Repeat on the other side.

Place the text rub-on transfers on the lower-left section of the card and the flower rub-ons near the right-hand ribbon.

Best Friends

LINDA BEESON

BLANK CARD: K & Company • PATTERNED PAPERS AND STICKER: Bo-Bunny Press • ALPHABET RUB-ON TRANSFERS: Making Memories

That friend who has stuck with you through it all will love this bright, cheery card. Using a variety of coordinated papers makes it fun to create.

Unfold the blank fold-over card and trace the shape onto the yellow patterned paper. Cut out the shape and glue it to the outside of the card. Ink the edges of the card with the brown chalk pad.

Tear a piece of red patterned paper to approximately 1¾" (4.5cm) wide. Ink the torn edges with brown chalk. Glue the strip to the bottom fold of the card, then trim the edges flush with the card sides.

Tear the top and bottom edges of the *best friends* sticker. Ink the edges with brown chalk. Adhere the sticker to the center of the red strip.

Cut a circle of pink patterned paper to fit the round metal tag, and glue it to the tag. Use rub-on letters to spell *luv U*. Glue the tag to the right of the sticker.

Punch two ½" (1.3cm) circles from the red patterned paper. Use the hole punch to punch a hole in the center of each circle. Punch a hole in the center of the top card flap, about ½" (1.3cm) from the edge. Insert an eyelet into one of the circles, then through the hole in the card; set the eyelet. Close the flap of the card and mark a spot ½" (1.3cm) down from the edge of the flap. Punch a hole here. Insert the second eyelet through the red circle, then through the second hole. Before setting the eyelet, tuck the ribbon under the red circle. Set the eyelet, catching the ribbon to secure it.

Friendship

LINDA BEESON

WHAT YOU'LL NEED

- brown cardstock
- green cardstock
- white cardstock
- flowered paper
- 12" (30cm) piece of pink and brown ribbon
- brown ink pad
- scissors or other cutting tool
- ruler
- bone folder (optional)
- sewing machine or needle with brown thread (optional)
- small flower punch
- 1/8" (3mm) hole punch
- glue stick or other adhesive
- font: Enviro

This sweet card can easily be made into a miniature book, filled with all the things that make your friend special. Just tuck a few pieces of paper inside before you sew the spine.

To each of us friendship has a different meaning. For all of us it is a gift.

Cut two pieces from the brown cardstock: 5" x 6" (13cm x 15cm) and 5" (13cm) square. Measure 1" (2.5cm) from a short end of the larger piece and score. Fold the edge over, then slip the smaller piece of cardstock under the fold.

Cut a ½" x 5" (1.3cm x 13cm) piece of the flowered paper and ink the edges with the brown ink pad. Glue the patterned piece to green cardstock. Trim the green cardstock to leave a narrow border on the long sides of the patterned paper. Ink the edges of the cardstock. Glue this layered piece on the flap on the front of the card, then sew around the inside edges of the patterned paper if desired to create a decorative spine.

Punch three evenly spaced holes ½" (1.3cm) in from the folded edge of the card. Cut three pieces of ribbon to approximately 4" (10cm) each and thread through the holes. Tie each ribbon in a knot.

Cut three 1" (2.5cm) squares from the flowered paper and ink the edges. Glue each onto green cardstock, and trim the cardstock to leave a narrow border; ink the edges.

Cut a ¼" (6mm) strip of green cardstock, ink the edges and glue about 1" (2.5cm) from the right edge of the card. Glue the three squares onto the strip, positioning them on end. Punch two flowers from white cardstock and two 1/8" (3mm) circles for centers from green cardstock. Glue the centers to the flowers, then glue the flowers between the squares.

Print the text in a rectangle shape on white cardstock. Trim the paper and ink the edges. Glue this piece to green cardstock and trim the cardstock to leave a narrow border. Ink the edges of the cardstock and glue to the front of the card as shown.

Leaving Footprints

KELLY ANNE GRUNDHAUSER

WHAT YOU'LL NEED

- pale green cardstock
- library pocket
- flower rubber stamp
- shoe rubber stamp
- 3¾" (9.5cm) piece of brown flowered ribbon
- text rub-on transfer
- silver flower charm
- brown ink pad
- brown marker
- yellow colored pencil
- scissors or other cutting tool
- ruler
- bone folder (optional)
- glue stick or other adhesive
- green glitter glue
- craft glue

Let your true friends know they stay in your heart wherever you go. The pocket and pull-out tag are perfect for a cheerful note or maybe a photo.

Cut the green cardstock to 8½" x 5½" (22cm x 14cm). Score and fold to create a card that's 5½" x 4¼" (14cm x 11cm). Stamp the flower image randomly over the front of the card in brown ink. Stamp the flowers on the inside flap of the library pocket, then color in the flowers on the flap with the brown marker.

Cut a tag measuring 3" x 4" (7.6cm x 10cm) from the green cardstock, and round the edges with scissors. With the brown ink pad, ink the edges of the front of the card, the library pocket and the tag.

Apply the text rub-on transfer to the front of the pocket. Glue the ribbon near the bottom of the pocket, then trim the ends flush with the pocket. Stamp the shoe just above the ribbon with brown ink, then embellish it with yellow colored pencil and green glitter glue.

Glue the pocket to the center of the card. Use craft glue to attach the charm to the center of the green tag and insert the tag in the pocket.

MANY PEOPLE WILL WALK IN AND OUT OF YOUR LIFE, BUT ONLY *true friends* WILL LEAVE FOOTPRINTS IN YOUR HEART.
ELEANOR ROOSEVELT

BTW › by the way ‹

WITH A DIFFERENT BACKGROUND STAMP AND SENTIMENT, YOU CAN USE THIS CARD FOR ANY OCCASION—A BIRTHDAY, CHRISTMAS OR A BABY SHOWER. SLIP A GIFT CARD IN THE POCKET AND YOU'RE GOOD TO GO.

A Real Friend
STACEY STAMITOLES

- dark periwinkle cardstock
- striped paper
- dot-patterned paper
- door-handle embellishment
- text sticker
- 6 star brads
- 6 paper flowers
- scissors or other cutting tool
- ruler
- bone folder (optional)
- glue stick or other adhesive
- glue dots

CARDSTOCK: Hero Arts • PATTERNED PAPERS: My Mind's Eye • DOOR HANDLE: 7gypsies • TEXT STICKER: Die Cuts With a View • BRADS: Accent Depot • PAPER FLOWERS: Prima

A real friend is a jewel when things are going well, but she's even more precious when things aren't so smooth. Let her know you're there to lean on or thank her for being your rock.

Cut the cardstock to 8½" x 5½" (22cm x 14cm). Score and fold the center to create a card that's 4¼" x 5½" (11cm x 14cm).

Cut the striped paper to 4" x 5¼" (10cm x 13cm). Pierce the door-handle embellishment through the right side.

From the left-over cardstock, cut two strips measuring ½" x 4¼" (1.3cm x 10.8cm). Cut the dot-patterned paper to 2½" x 3³/₈" (6.4cm x 8.6cm). Adhere the text sticker to the lower part of the dotted paper. Glue the cardstock strips behind the dotted paper, then glue the layered piece to the striped paper.

Insert a brad into the center of each flower, then attach the flowers at the top and bottom edges of the dots paper with glue dots. Glue the striped paper to the front of the card.

BTW
by the way

SAVE LEFT-OVER PAPER AND CARDSTOCK FOR FUTURE CARDS IN A FILING SYSTEM BY COLOR OR JUST IN A STORAGE BIN OR BASKET. IT'S GREAT TO FIND THE PERFECT SCRAP OF CARDSTOCK YOU NEED WITHOUT HAVING TO CUT INTO A WHOLE NEW PIECE.

What You'll Need

It doesn't take much to get started making greeting cards. One trip through the house collecting the art supplies you have and a quick trip to the local craft, stamp or scrapbook store should produce all the supplies you need. If you're unfamiliar with the tools and materials used in the book, these pages will help it all make sense.

Paper

There are two kinds of paper used predominantly in card making. The first is **CARDSTOCK**, a heavyweight paper that is often used as the base of a card. Cardstock is available in solid colors, with or without a bit of texture, as well as patterned designs. A huge array of colors is available, so you're sure to find just the right color for your project.

PATTERNED PAPER is the other type of paper featured often in the projects in this book. Generally, patterned paper is as heavy as good copier paper. It can be used in small sections as an accent to your design, or you can use it to cover the entire front of the card. If you haven't been to a scrapbook or craft store lately, you will be blown away by the variety of patterned papers available. Once you start collecting it, you may never stop.

Cutting Tools

Good ol' scissors can always be used to cut paper, but there are some tools available that are much easier to use. **SLIDE PAPER TRIMMERS,** found at craft and scrapbook stores, make quick work of cutting straight lines. Many models are large enough to accommodate 12" x 12" (30cm x 30cm) sheets of paper and may come with a scoring blade as well.

Another option for cutting straight lines is to use a **CRAFT KNIFE, METAL-EDGED RULER, AND CUTTING MAT.** A metal edge allows you to run the knife along the edge of the ruler without damaging it, and the cutting mat will protect your work surface.

Once you get beyond straight lines, you'll find that small **DETAIL SCISSORS** come in awfully handy. These will allow you to trim neatly around a flower on a piece of patterned paper or to cut a simple wavy line.

SHAPE CUTTERS AND PAPER PUNCHES allow you to cut smooth-edged shapes in a snap. Shape cutters come with a special cutting tool and templates to make circles, ovals, hearts and more. For smaller circles and other shapes, a paper punch works well.

Adhesives

There are tons of adhesives available, many that work best in specific situations. If you're just getting started, all you need is a **GLUE STICK OR DOUBLE-SIDED TAPE** for attaching paper to paper, and either **CRAFT GLUE OR GLUE DOTS** for attaching heavier or more dimensional items to paper.

Stamping Supplies

Rubber stamps and ink pads are terrific tools for adding images and color to your cards. Rubber stamps of every kind are available at craft, scrapbook and stamping stores, including ones with outlined images, fitting sentiments and simple solid shapes. Having even a few stamps on hand with images or words that fit your style will help you if you ever get stuck for card ideas.

Ink pads come in different types to suit different situations. If you're stamping on something other than paper or if you'll be coloring in the image with watercolors, use a permanent ink pad. If you want to emboss a stamped image with embossing powder, use a pigment ink pad. In most other cases, however, just about any ink pad will do the trick.

Adding color to stamped images is fun and can be done with colored pencils, watercolor pencils, markers—whatever suits your fancy.

Continue through the next few pages to see some of these supplies—and more—in action!

How'd She Do That?

Scoring and folding a card

Premade card bases are readily available at craft, stamp and scrapbook stores, but if you don't mind making your own, you'll find your card base options will grow exponentially. (Remember all that great cardstock we talked about earlier?)

1 To score a card, measure to find the center and make marks at this point at the top and bottom of the card. Line up a ruler on the marks and score by running a bone folder along the ruler from top to bottom.

2 Fold the card along the score line, then use the bone folder again to make the crease nice and crisp.

Punching out shapes

Paper punches make cutting out small shapes so easy. A collection of a few geometric-shape dies and maybe a flower punch or two will add much to your card creations. And should your punches ever get dull, punch a piece of aluminum foil a few times to sharpen the blade.

In most instances, you can simply insert the paper, place the punch flat on your work surface and punch away. If, however, you want to punch a specific area out of patterned paper, turn the punch over to find the right spot. Then punch by pressing the punch side on the work surface (if you're really talented) or hold the paper in place and turn the punch over and punch as normal.

Using rub-on transfers

Rub-on transfers are super cool! If you haven't tried them, you simply must. They come in sheets, like stickers, but when the image is rubbed onto the paper, it looks just like it's part of the surface.

1 With scissors, cut out just the image you want to transfer.

2 Remove the white paper backing, and place the image on the paper. Using the stick that comes with the transfers or a bone folder, rub the plastic backing, making sure to rub over each part of the image.

3 Slowly peel off the plastic backing to reveal the transfer. If any part of the image isn't completely transferred, put the plastic back down and rub over it again.

Using a sewing machine

Adding a little stitching to cards isn't hard. Whether you purchase a small craft sewing machine or use your mother's old hand-me-down, you will find that sewing a few simple stitches can really add a lot of character to your paper projects. Take a few moments to read the instructions for your machine—at least how to thread the needle and bobbin—then, have fun playing!

Feed the paper (or fabric) slowly as you sew; this will help you to maintain control of your stitching. For straight lines, use the edge of the presser foot or guidelines to the right of the presser foot to help you along.

Using a rubber stamp

Rubber stamps provide a quick and easy way to put just the right image or sentiment on your cards. No special skills are needed, but the following pointers will make the process go a bit smoother. If you are puzzled about what kind of ink pad to use, turn to page 85 for some guidelines.

1 Lightly tap the stamp onto the ink pad. Pressing the stamp into the pad can overink the stamp and result in a messy image.

2 Press the stamp firmly onto the paper, or whatever you're stamping. It sometimes helps to stand as you press. Do not rock the stamp as you press, however, or you may smear the image.

3 Lift the stamp up and away to reveal the image. Voilá!

BTW
by the way

IF YOU'RE STAMPING A LARGE IMAGE OR IF YOU WANT TO INK ONLY PART OF A STAMP, TURN THE STAMP OVER AND TAP THE PAD ONTO THE RUBBER.

Adding color to a stamped image

Once your image is stamped, you can use it as is or add a bit of color to it. Coloring in a stamped outline may bring back fond memories of using your favorite coloring books, but maybe with a slightly more sophisticated look. Colored pencils, markers, watercolor pencils or regular watercolors are just a few of the mediums you can use.

When using colored pencils to color a stamped image, a dull tip will give you a softer look than a sharpened tip. You can also rub your finger over the colored image to soften it a bit more.

Inking paper edges

Whether a piece of paper is stamped or not, you may want to ink the edges to give it a special effect. To soften the edges of the paper so that it will blend into the rest of your design, use an ink color similar to that of the paper in your design. To make a piece of paper stand out from the design, ink the edges with a contrasting color. No matter your need, inking the edges will do the trick!

1 To simply ink the edges of a piece of paper, lightly tap the edges onto an ink pad. If you'd like a little more color, press it harder into the ink pad.

2 For a lot of color on the front of the paper, smear the paper with the ink pad. Use a light hand and gradually add more color if you like.

Patterns You Can Use

Groovy Chick

Use this pattern at 100% to make the card on page 68.

Showers of Happiness

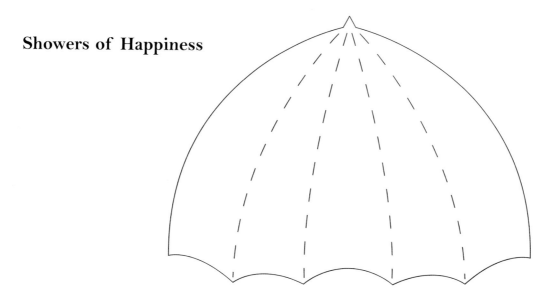

Use this pattern at 100% to make the card on page 49.

A True Friend Tells You...

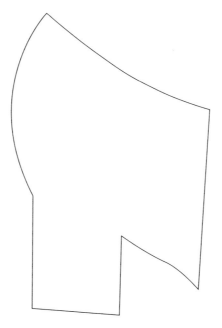

Use this pattern at 100% to make the card on page 74.

Vintage Girl

Use this pattern at 100% to make the card on page 34.

Where'd She Get That?

The products used in this book can be found at your local scrapbook, rubber stamp or craft store. If you aren't able to find a particular product, contact the manufacturer listed below for a retailer in your area.

7gypsies
877-749-7797
www.7gypsies.com

A Charming Place
www.acharmingplace.com

All Night Media
see Plaid Enterprises, Inc.

A Muse Artstamps
877-783-4882
www.amuseartstamps.com

Accent Depot
see Hot Off the Press

American Crafts
801-226-0747
www.americancrafts.com

Autumn Leaves
800-588-6707
www.autumnleaves.com

Avery Dennison Corporation
800-462-8379
www.avery.com

Basic Grey
801-544-1116
www.basicgrey.com

Bazzill Basics Paper
480-558-8557
www.bazzillbasics.com

Berwick Offray, LLC
800-344-5533
www.offray.com

Bo-Bunny Press
801-771-4010
www.bobunny.com

Canson, Inc.
800-628-9283
www.canson-us.com

Carolee's Creations & Co. LLC
435-563-1100
www.caroleescreations.com

Chatterbox, Inc.
888-416-6260
www.chatterboxinc.com

Clearsnap, Inc.
888-448-4862
www.clearsnap.com

Colorbok, Inc.
800-366-4660
www.colorbok.com

ColorBox
see Clearsnap, Inc.

Crafts U Love, LTD
www.craftsulove.co.uk

Creative Imaginations
800-942-6487
www.cigift.com

C.R. Gibson
800-243-6004
www.crgibson.com

DaFont
www.dafont.com

Daisy D's Paper Company
888-601-8955
www.daisydspaper.com

Deluxe Designs
480-497-9005
www.deluxecuts.com
Die Cuts With a View
801-224-6766
www.dcwv.com

DMD Industries, Inc.
800-805-9890
www.dmdind.com

Doodlebug Design Inc.
877-800-9190
www.doodlebug.ws

EK Success, Ltd.
800-524-1349
www.eksuccess.com

Family Treasures, Inc.
949-290-0872
www.familytreasures.com

Fibers By The Yard
800-760-8901
www.fibersbytheyard.com

Fiskars
866-348-5661
www.fiskars.com

Flair Designs
888-546-9990
www.flairdesignsinc.com

Font Diner
www.fontdiner.com

FoofaLa
402-330-3208
www.foofala.com

Glue Dots International
888-688-7131
www.gluedots.com

Heidi Grace Designs
866-894-3434
www.heidigrace.com

Heidi Swapp Advantus Corporation
904-482-0092
www.heidiswapp.com

Hero Arts
800-822-4376
www.heroarts.com

Hirschberg Schultz & Co., Inc.
800-221-8640

Hot Off the Press
800-227-9595
www.b2b.hotp.com

Jacquard Products/ Rupert, Gibbon &
Spider, Inc.
800-442-0455
www.jacquardproducts.com

Jewelry & Handbag Warehouse
www.jewelry-handbag.com

JudiKins
310-515-1115
www.judikins.com

K&Company
888-244-2083
www.kandcompany.com

Karen Foster Design
801-451-9779
www.karenfosterdesign.com

KI Memories
972-243-5595
www.kimemories.com

Lasting Impressions
800-936-2677
www.lastingimpressions.com

Li'l Davis Designs
949-838-0344
www.lildavisdesigns.com

Magic Mesh
651-345-6374
www.magicmesh.com

Making Memories
801-294-0430
www.makingmemories.com

Mara-Mi, Inc.
800-627-2648
www.mara-mi.com

Marvy Uchida/Uchida of America, Corp.
800-541-5877
www.uchida.com

May Arts
800-442-3950
www.mayarts.com

McGill, Inc.
800-982-9884
www.mcgillinc.com

Me & My Big Ideas
949-583-2065
www.meandmybigideas.com

Memories Forever
see Westrim Crafts

MOD-my own design
303-641-8680
www.mod-myowndesign.com

My Mind's Eye
866-989-0320
www.frame-ups.com

My Sentiments Exactly!
719-260-6001
www.sentiments.com

NRN Designs
800-421-6958
www.nrndesigns.com

Offray
see Berwick Offray

The Paper Company
800-426-8989
www.thepapercompany.com

Paper Salon
952-445-6878
www.papersalon.com

The Paper Studio
480-557-5700
www.paperstudio.com

Paperbilities
see Westrim Crafts

Papershapers
see EK Success

Pebbles Inc.
801-235-1520
www.pebblesinc.com

Plaid Enterprises, Inc.
800-842-4197
www.plaidonline.com

PM Designs
888-595-2887
www.designsbypm.com

Prima Marketing, Inc.
909-627-5532
www.primamarketinginc.com

ProvoCraft
800-937-7686
www.provocraft.com

Putting on the Ritz
425-392-3358
www.stampingontheritz.com

Queen & Co.
858-613-7858
www.queenandcompany.com

Quickutz, Inc.
888-702-1146
www.quickutz.com

Ranger Industries, Inc.
732-389-3535
www.rangerink.com

Rob and Bob Studio
see ProvoCraft

Royal & Langnickel/Royal Brush Mfg.
800-247-2211
www.royalbrush.com

Sassafras Lass
801-269-1331
www.sassafraslass.com

Savvy Stamps
866-447-2889
www.savvystamps.com

SEI, Inc.
800-333-3279
www.shopsei.com

Self Addressed
866-300-7474
www.self-addressed.com

Shortcuts
see Crafts U Love, LTD

Swarovski
800-426-3088
www.swarovski.com

Two Peas in a Bucket, Inc.
888-896-7327
www.twopeasinabucket.com

Westrim Crafts
800-727-2727
www.westrimcrafts.com

Wordsworth
719-282-3495
www.wordsworthstamps.com

Zsiage
718-224-1976
www.zsiage.com

Index

Index of Cards

Check out these other great books from North Light

Judi Watanabe, Alison Eads and Laurie Dewberry

Retro Mania! shows you how to make swell papercrafts using hot images and graphics from your favorite decades. You'll find 50 projects featuring popular decade-inspired motifs, from the swellegant 40s and fabulous 50s to the psychedelic 60s and groovy 70s. You'll love the stylish handmade cards, scrapbook pages and gift ideas with tips on customizing the projects to your personal swingin' taste.

**ISBN 1-58180-746-5 . . . ISBN-13 9781581807462
PAPERBACK . . . 96 PAGES . . . 33418**

Heidi Boyd

Whether you're a complete beginner or a seasoned crafter, *Simply Beautiful Greeting Cards* shows you how to create personalized greeting cards for every occasion. You'll find cards that are great for holidays, birthdays, weddings and "just because." With 50 different quick and easy cards to choose from, you'll be eager to show your family and friends how much you care with style and flair. In addition to the wide array of cards, you'll find a helpful section on basic tools and materials as well as a treasure trove of papercrafting tips and tricks.

**ISBN 1-58180-564-0 . . . ISBN-13 9781581805642
PAPERBACK . . . 128 PAGES . . . 33019**

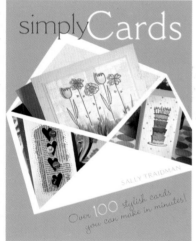

Sally Traidman

From birthdays to holidays and for all occasions in between, turn to the bright and breezy style of the cards featured in *Simply Cards*. The candy colors, spring brights and retro hues of these cards give them a young, fresh and playful look that's sure to appeal to anyone who receives one of these simple and graphic missives. You'll get maximum yield for minimum time with the cards in this book—just a few basic papercrafting techniques combined with a little rubber stamping, and voilá, the perfect card.

**ISBN 1-58180-674-4
ISBN-13 97818581806748
PAPERBACK . . . 128 PAGES . . . 33260**

Alison Eads

The Artful Card showcases over 25 gorgeous cards and keepsakes made with collage techniques using printed papers, embellishments and found objects. With her unique, romantic style and simple yet clever techniques, Alison Eads brings the hottest trends in scrapbooking to the cardmaking world. Whether you're making a romantic card for your someone special, or you just want to send a friend or family member a handmade message to show you care, you're sure to find just the right thing here.

**ISBN 1-58180-680-9 . . . ISBN-13 9781581806809
PAPERBACK . . . 128 PAGES . . . 33269**

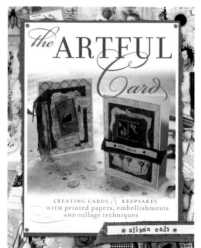

These books and other fine North Light titles are available at your local craft or scrapbook store, bookstore or from online suppliers.